Creating Space

Creating Space

MY LIFE AND WORK IN INDIGENOUS EDUCATION

VERNA J. KIRKNESS

UMP
University of Manitoba Press

Creating Space: My Life and Work in Indigenous Education
© Verna J. Kirkness 2013

22   21   20   19   18   4   5   6   7   8

University of Manitoba Press
Winnipeg, Manitoba, Canada
Treaty 1 Territory
uofmpress.ca

Cataloguing data available from Library and Archives Canada
ISBN 978-0-88755-743-9 (PAPER)
ISBN 978-0-88755-444-5 (PDF)
ISBN 978-0-88755-445-2 (EPUB)

Cover and interior design: Jess Koroscil
Cover photo: Ian McCausland

Printed in Canada

The University of Manitoba Press acknowledges the financial support for
its publication program provided by the Government of Canada through
the Canada Book Fund, the Canada Council for the Arts, the Manitoba
Department of Sport, Culture, and Heritage, the Manitoba Arts Council,
and the Manitoba Book Publishing Tax Credit.

Funded by the Government of Canada   Canadä

CONTENTS

Photographs follow pages 66 and 162

LIST OF PHOTOGRAPHS

Unless otherwise noted, photographs are used by courtesy of the author.

ACKNOWLEDGEMENTS

I AM MOST INDEBTED TO CAROLYN KENNY for her faith in me and her constant encouragement to get this book done. It has been several years in the making and there were many times that I wanted to give up on it, and each time she managed to get me back to the drawing board. She is the reason that I have finally completed it and it will be out there for all who are interested in Aboriginal education and the life of a Cree woman. Thank you, Carolyn, you are a dear sister.

I am thankful to my friend, Pat McManus, who has journeyed with me much of the way in Aboriginal education, for helping me remember certain experiences that we shared, for reading drafts of this book and assuring me that it is a story that should be told. Without her encouragement and assistance, the completion of the book would have been more difficult.

Another person so essential to this effort is Cory Whitney, who provided me with the technical assistance I required. I know very little about computers. I thank him for his patience and willingness to come to my rescue so many times over the years that I have been working on this book.

A number of the photos shown came from the collection of the late Julia Spence (McGill). I'm thankful for her love and support. I also want to thank Patricia Beyer, Dorothy (Fahner) McKay, Pat McManus, and Peg Klesner for contributing to the photo section.

Foreword

IN MID NOVEMBER the residents of Fisher River Cree Nation in Manitoba begin to feel the chilly breezes as they sweep down from the far north. Prairie grasses, birch and pine trees, and white poplars bend and sway from new winds that carry a message of winter to come. Skies are clear—Manitoba being the place with the clearest blue skies year round in all of Canada. However, great grey owls and peregrine falcons know, just like the people on the reserve, that snowy blizzards will soon be travelling on the open landscape.

On just such an anticipatory day in November, one of Manitoba's favourite Native daughters was born. Verna Jane Kirkness was born on November 20th, 1935. Destined to be a world traveller who carried a message of hope, enthusiasm, tenacity, integrity, and renewal, Verna Jane would not disappoint.

In this book you will learn another story—a story that is indeed "in context" of a life lived with sacrifice, honour, dedication, vision, and intelligence. It is also a story of joys and sorrows, challenges and misgivings, burning questions, successes and failures. It is the story of a Cree woman's experience of becoming a leader and following the guidance of her intuition and her Creator—a momentum that propelled her as a visionary.

As you turn these pages, you will get to know Verna the daughter, the aunt, the sister, the lover, the friend. You will sense the laughter in her friendships. And you will feel the spiritual nature of her journey. This is a story that only Verna could tell.

Yet the story is also an important Canadian, Aboriginal, and international story about teaching and learning. Verna takes us through her early experiences as a teacher, her commitment to teach in a "Native" way, her political efforts to advance the cause of Aboriginal education through advocating for *Indian Control of Indian Education*, her initiatives on behalf of students to create "a home away from home," and her ongoing presence at our gatherings to inspire and motivate us to have the courage to take up the challenges to make this a better world—and much more.

Because of her accomplishments, Verna Jane is a stunning role model for all of those who aspire to lead. If you have never had an opportunity to have a good laugh with Verna, I suggest you make it a priority.

It has been my pleasure and my honour to walk with her in the creation of this book. And every minute, every chapter, every draft, every conversation, has kept my complete attention. It will be the same for you. So get ready. This is not just a story. It is a world.

Carolyn Kenny

Preface

IT WAS SEVERAL YEARS AGO that I thought of writing a book about my life as an educator and a person who grew up on an Indian reserve. I feel very privileged to have been a part of many advances that have occurred in Aboriginal education during my lifetime. This is a story of my family, my jobs, my bosses, my colleagues, my friends, my relationships, and the evolving changes in Aboriginal education, all intertwined as they occurred in my life.

Being a teacher had been my childhood dream and when I became a teacher I had no further aspirations. I loved being an elementary school teacher. When I was presented with an opportunity to assume more responsibility, I did not readily accept the change. Persuasion has its place and I succumbed, taking on the challenge of being the Senior Teacher, in charge of twelve teachers and over three hundred children, at the Rossville Indian Residential and Day School in Norway House. This was the turning point in my life that would take me to places I never dreamed of as a child.

From there on, a pattern developed, and my life became one of an educator, as opportunities arose that involved advancing Aboriginal education in different ways; creating space, as it were, for our people. One of the few "first wave" Aboriginal academics, as Jo-ann Archibald called us, I was a pioneer in the field and numerous opportunities opened up for me to break new ground. I went on to experience several firsts over the course of my career. This is what prompted me to use the title, "Creating Space." Each new challenge opened doors for Aboriginal people in academia. For example, my appointment as the first Supervisor of Schools for a northern school division signified an emerging awareness that Aboriginal issues had to be addressed in schools. Being the first Cross-Cultural Consultant with the responsibility of addressing Aboriginal issues indicated the voices of our people had been heard and a provincial Department of Education had acknowledged that changes were required to make the curriculum better suited to Aboriginal children. As the first Director of Education for both the Manitoba Indian Brotherhood (Assembly of Manitoba Chiefs) and the National Indian Brotherhood (Assembly of First Nations), I had the opportunity to work in policy making that signalled that Aboriginal people were taking charge of the education of their children. The landmark policy of Indian Control of Indian Education has been one of the greatest achievements of Aboriginal people in our history. At the University of British Columbia, starting in the early 1980s, where I worked first at the undergraduate level followed by graduate studies, earmarks a time when universities across Canada were beginning to address the need for better access and support for Aboriginal students. My story must be understood within these shifting contexts, but it also provides a context for you to see the shifts as they occurred, through the eyes of an Aboriginal educator.

When I look back on this experience, I see it as a snowball effect. Each new opportunity grew out of the previous one and I needed this progression to meet each new challenge I undertook.

My approach to writing this book was to do it almost entirely from memory, as if telling you a story over a cup of tea. When telling a story, quite often we stray off the topic to add a related event—but eventually we get on with the story. I am guilty of that, and if it were to be a scholarly treatise, I would have to use a different approach. In these pages you will find what stood out in my mind about my life experience.

Education has been my life. As a child I loved school; as an adult I worked in various capacities in education from 1954 to 1993; and since I retired, I have had interesting projects to work on that include the revival and preservation of our languages, heading a consultation team that led to the creation of a new university college in northern Manitoba, and initiating a university program for Aboriginal scholars to attain PhDs at the University of Manitoba.

My intention for this book is to bring a sense of the history of Aboriginal education in Canada to the readers, especially the young Aboriginal people who rely on our own stories—oral histories—to track our progress through the years. A constant theme in my talks has been that "You must know the past, to understand the present, to plan for the future." I hope my story will give you a useful window on the past.

NOTE ON TERMINOLOGY

You will note that I use the terms Indian, Native, Native Indian, Aboriginal, and Indigenous interchangeably throughout the book, depending on the popular term used at certain time periods. I choose to use Indigenous in the title because it is inclusive of all first peoples whether they live in Canada, United States, New Zealand, Australia, Hawaii, or Taiwan.

Creating Space

CHAPTER ONE

My Family

MY ONLY REAL ASPIRATION WAS to become a teacher, particularly a teacher among my own people. I was born with a love for school. I can trace my fascination with school back to some of my earliest memories. Before I was even old enough to start school, I would often sneak away from our house, which was right next to the school, and knock on the school door. The teacher would tell me I was too young to go to school and I must go back home. I could see the kids playing at recess time and I dearly wanted to join them.

When I finally started school, and learned nursery rhymes, I would translate them into Cree and recite them to my mother when I got home. One was "Three little kittens who lost their mittens" (nisto possessuk-ke wanihawuk-otustisuk). My mother got a real kick out of this, and whenever we had visitors she would have me repeat these nursery rhymes in Cree to them and they would have a good laugh. When I think about this now, I wonder if I may have been compensating for the lack of any relevance in what I was learning.

I hated to miss school. It was typical for children to be kept home on laundry days to help with the laundry since it entailed hauling water or snow, heating it in a big boiler, using a washboard, and finally hanging the clothes out on a clothesline to dry. My mother tried the same with me but I fussed so much that she'd say, "Oh, go to school then!"

When I started school in 1941, we had only two classrooms. The junior room had forty children or so in grades one and two and the senior room had about thirty in grades three to eight. The reason that there were so many children in the first two grades is that many entered school at that time only knowing the Cree language. To accommodate these children there was a strange system of being placed as a Beginner upon entry, then on to Class A, Class B, and Class C, and on to grade one junior and grade one senior. You progressed according to how proficient you became in speaking English. There was no such program as "English as a Second Language" and teachers had no idea what to do except to expect the children to pick up English somehow. Some children actually spent a whole year as Beginners and spent another year or more getting to grade one. Those of us who could speak English could progress more quickly.

I have no idea if our curriculum or textbooks were up to date, but I suspect they were not. The schools were not bound to follow the provincial curriculum in those days because they were federal schools run by the Department of Indian Affairs. Nor do I remember ever learning about the history of Indian people, hearing any stories of famous Indians, or seeing Indian children in any books. Our primary reader was *Highroads to Reading* with "Jerry and Jane," which featured a white, urban, nuclear family whose father went to work in an office and whose mother stayed home with the children. Jerry and Jane were always spotless. We had a few books on a bookshelf in the back of the classroom. I'm sure these were donated by some church. I remember that one of our teachers would read a chapter from a book right after lunch each day. I loved the stories and would rush back from lunch not to be late because the story began right at one o'clock. *Black Beauty* and *Heidi* were two of my favourites. I read them over and over again after the teacher finished the story. The library books and textbooks were often covered with brown paper, I assume to keep them from getting soiled.

School was my passion. It did not matter, really, if the teacher was strict or lenient, though the former was more often the case, as that is what was expected of them. We did not know what their qualifications were. I suspect that many were permit teachers, since reserve schools were in rural and remote areas and would be considered schools of last resort. All the teachers were Caucasian and, as I learned later, from rural areas of Manitoba, usually farming communities. I was told that one of the teachers in the early years was Indian, but she anglicized her name and did not identify with us. That was sad, since she would have been an invaluable role model. I believe that on the whole we had caring teachers. When I talk to people my age, they say some of the teachers were mean. I don't remember that, and my love for school was not deterred by any of them.

I have no idea who my biological father was; I mention this because it did have an effect on my life. In all my years, it never caused me any self-doubts or anxiety. I am sure the reason for this is that at four years of age I was blessed with a father who loved and cared for me as his own. One might say that he chose me as his daughter. Fred Kirkness married my mother in November 1939. I don't recall the actual wedding but I do remember that during their courtship he was very nice to me and I really liked him. He may have been the first male love of my life, though I did adore my Uncle Jim, who was my mother's brother. I have no idea if I was privy to hearing the proposal or heard my mother tell my grandmother about it, but I have been told that I said to my mother, "If you don't marry him, I will." Fred Kirkness, who became my father, truly remained a person for whom I held a great deal of love and respect. If the saying is true that girls marry men that are like their fathers, then I have never found such a man that could measure up to him. Not only was he a big man, six feet tall and over two hundred pounds, but he was also gentle, kind, patient, and fun.

I think it strange that now at my advanced age I am somewhat curious to know who my biological father was. It is not because of a need to know my identity, as I am very aware and proud of being a Cree woman, but it is rather a curiosity to understand myself and to understand what part his genes may have played in the kind of person I turned out to be. Why did my mother never tell me who he was? Why did I not confront her to find out? My mother was twenty-four years old when I was born. It is not as if she was a teenager or a drunk and did not know who my father was. My mother was never a drinker. I know that even one bottle of beer would make her sick. Anyway, for some reason, she chose to let it remain a secret and I let her do it.

When I was born on November 20, 1935, my mother, Gladys Grace Williams, was living with her bother Jim at his home in Fisher River, Manitoba. She had been in Kenora, Ontario, helping her sister, my Aunt Harriet, take care of her young children. My mother returned to Fisher River to have me. A Cree midwife helped bring me into the world. This led me to believe that I was conceived in Kenora. I was ten years old when my mother returned to Kenora for the first time since she left there when she was expecting me. She took my sister, Mary Ann, and me with her to visit my Aunt Harriet and her family. My aunt and her Hungarian-born husband had six children by that time. I remember going with my Aunt Harriet and my mom to a restaurant where a man joined us for lunch. He seemed very attentive toward me and asked me questions about where I lived and what I like to do. He was Chinese. While we never saw him again, I wondered if he was my father and, perhaps, his circumstances did not allow for further contact. I am so often mistaken for being Asian by Asian people and others that the possibility of having Chinese heritage remains with me. As an adult, in my travels through Kenora, I wonder if I might have siblings living there. I will probably never know the origin of my birth, as those who could have told me have now passed on.

Upon my birth, I had a mother, a maternal grandmother, several uncles, and aunts. I always had a special relationship with my Uncle Jim, with whom we lived. The four of us were my nuclear family until the age of four when my mother married Fred Kirkness. My mother was a Williams and I was registered as Verna Jane Williams. My grannie, my mother's mother, was Mary Ann McKay, because she married for a second time. I have wonderful memories of time spent with my grandmother. Though she was bedridden, she could keep me amused with her legends and stories. I am not sure what she was suffering from but I now believe it may have been a kind of cancer. Since I spent a great deal of time with her those first four years of my life, I learned a lot from her as we communicated in Cree. She gave me the invaluable gift of learning my mother tongue that has sustained me all of my life as a Cree woman. She was my constant companion and my mother was her caregiver. My Uncle Jim was the provider for our family. Grannie died shortly after my mother married Fred Kirkness.

The marriage brought with it others who would become my family. Fred (strangely enough, that is what I always called him, never Dad) was a widower with four children from his previous marriage. Upon his wife Olive's death, the youngest child, Ida, went to live with her paternal grandparents and Margaret went with the maternal grandparents. Maria Jane, the oldest, and Clarence were in boarding school in Brandon. Since they did not live with us, I did not regard them as siblings. Ida, who was five years older than me, was a bit jealous of me because her dad now lived with us. Later, we would become very close and treated one another as real sisters, though by blood we were not related at all. Ida gave me my first wristwatch when I was around thirteen and helped me through summer school at United College. She married Bill Cooksley, a high-school teacher, and they moved to Sault Ste. Marie, Ontario. We continued to remain very close, and they were the family members who came to be with me when I received an honorary doctorate from Mount Saint Vincent University in Halifax in 1990. We were good friends and I was very sad when she succumbed in 1991 to the cancer she had been fighting for years.

My mother and dad (I always referred to him as my dad when speaking of him) went on to have several children. The first to be born was Rosalyn. She was four years younger than me. She suffered from epilepsy and was mostly in poor health. I helped to take care of her, as my mother was often alone because Dad had to be away during the fishing season. Maria Jane returned to the reserve, as she was in the late stages of tuberculosis. She was in her early twenties and had been working in Winnipeg. She died shortly after she returned home. A wake was held at the home of her paternal grandparents. Rosalyn was four years old, and we were sleeping upstairs while the wake was going on. Suddenly, I was aware that Rosalyn was not feeling well and that she had a nosebleed. I went downstairs to where the wake was to get my mother. The nosebleed got worse and others were trying to attend to her while Dad walked to the United Church, about two kilometres away, to get the minister to take Rosalyn to the hospital, fifteen kilometers away. The minister was the only one with a car on the reserve and he also dispensed medicine to the people. When he got there, the minister did not feel it was necessary to take her to the hospital just for a nosebleed. He instructed my dad on how to take care of her to stop the bleeding. During the night, Rosalyn passed away. It was a terrible time! Here they would be burying Maria Jane and now her half-sister had also died. My mother and dad were totally broken up by the deaths. My mother was unable to go to the funeral that day. Dad and the rest of the family attended. When the minister saw my Dad, he asked, "And how is the little girl, Mr. Kirkness?" Dad responded, "She died last night." The minister was taken aback. I was eight years old at the time and I felt the loss of Rosalyn deeply. I remember dreaming of her many times after she died.

At some point Clarence came to live with us for a while after he left boarding school, but he soon went away to work. Margaret settled in the Kenora area with her partner and children. Many years later, she returned to Fisher River to live in the personal care home, as she was no longer able to take care of herself due to an acute case of arthritis. She died after a short stay at the home. I remember that my mother was always good to Dad's first family. They visited us, and we all had pleasant times together.

Mary Ann was the next to be born and was just two years old when Rosalyn died. After her, Gladys Mae was born and lived only for a month. Darlene was born in 1947. Reggie was the last to be born in 1950. After Reggie, Mom had a miscarriage. If all the children had lived, I would have had six siblings in my family. Today, the only one alive is Mary Ann, who is six years younger than me. While I do not give it a lot of thought, I do realize that I have no full-blood siblings; in fact, I have no full-blood relatives.

I will always be grateful that I also inherited wonderful grandparents on the Kirkness side. They were very kind to me and treated me the same as their other grandchildren. Grannie Maria passed away in 1957 while I was teaching in Fisher River. Mooshoom (Jim) Kirkness lived to be 104 years old. He passed away in 1974. He was a great inspiration to me, as he took an interest in what I was doing. Referring to the fact that I was a teacher, he said to me one day, "You are still not as smart as your grandfather." He then pulled out a newsletter written in English and Cree syllabics and proceeded to read in both languages. He was certainly right, as I still have not mastered the Cree syllabics. He challenged me in a fun way.

Mooshoom had a very interesting life story and I decided that recording it would be my centennial project in 1967. I always loved visiting with him, as he had many interesting stories to tell me. Our conversations were always in Cree. I was working in Winnipeg as a guidance counsellor at the time and my good intentions did not materialize except for about three hours of tape. I have regretted since that I did not record his story.

In short, when my grandfather was only four years old, the family started out on a journey from York Factory to Norway House that would take three years because they could only travel in winter. The summer was for making pemmican and moccasins and other preparations for the winter journey by dog sled. They were going to Norway House for the signing of Treaty 5. When I recount this story, I usually say, "Needless to say, the treaty party had gone by the time they arrived." This meant that they would be regarded as non-treaty Indians and would not have the privileges of the Status Indians recognized by the federal government. Eventually they relocated from Norway House to Fisher Bay, a non-treaty settlement about six miles from Fisher River. Not until 1908, when the Norway House, Cross Lake, and Fisher River adhesion to Treaty 5 was signed, did the family (several children were born by then) become Status Indians. My grandfather was a signatory to the adhesion. When I first saw a copy of this document, I asked why he put an "X" instead of writing his name, as he was literate. He said, "They told me to." I learned much from my grandfather and had visited him just the day before his death, as it was during the Christmas break. At 104, his mind was clear to the end.

Besides these wonderful grandparents, I inherited many aunts, uncles, and cousins, as my dad had five brothers. To this day, I remain close to my cousins. On February 29, 2012, the last of my parents' generation, my Aunt Annie Kirkness, passed away at the age of 99. She had been the oldest resident at Fisher River.

My mother had two brothers and three sisters, all of whom are deceased. I remain close to several of these cousins, particularly my Aunt Harriet's family that I refer to as my Hungarian cousins. They were born and raised in Kenora, Ontario—and now live in Dryden, Thunder Bay, and Petrolia. A few of my cousins still live at Fisher River. The family I am closest to is the McKay family, who are my second cousins. Stanley McKay (Senior) was my mother's first cousin, as their mothers were sisters. From an early age, I spent time with this family of five siblings, some older and some younger than me.

In fact, Patsy and Doreen, who are older than me, guided me in my early stages of learning to walk. We get together regularly for casual visits or to celebrate various milestones.

While I did not know my biological father, I had a typical family, but there was one unforeseen effect resulting from my mysterious birth. My mother did not register me as a member of the Fisher River Band, even through it was customary for single mothers to register their children. Consequently, I fell into the category of being a non-Status Indian as far as the government was concerned. This would have a profound effect on my life.

Early in my life, I was aware of being excluded from certain benefits that Status Indians received early in life. One example was that I was the only one in our family who did not receive treaty money on Treaty Days. The five-dollar treaty payments are given out annually and payments remain the same today. Treaty time was an annual get-together when families and friends came for their treaty money and to enjoy several days of activity that included sports such as rowing competitions and baseball during the day and square dancing and jigging at night. At little stands you could buy all kinds of goodies such as hot dogs, ice cream, and soft drinks. It was the only time of year when we could get such rare treats as ice cream, bananas, and watermelon. My earliest memory of prices is when an ice-cream cone was five cents, soft drinks were seven cents, chocolate bars were six cents, and apples and oranges were five cents each. There were usually several makeshift shelters that served as restaurants that sold full-course meals including such fare as moose meat and fish. Treaty time holds wonderful memories for me as a child. It was an exciting time when families set up tents and remained together for several days. Among the temporary structures were one or more dance halls, as we called them. I wonder if they managed to cover their costs at ten cents a dance. A man would go around with a cap and the men had to make sure they had plenty of dimes for the night. I remember we got new clothes to wear. When you add it all up, it is easy to see that even with the prices of the day, five dollars did not go very far. But those who got it were five dollars richer than me.

After my mother's marriage we continued to live with my Uncle Jim. The house had one large room that served as a bedroom and living room warmed by a pot-bellied wood stove. Early on, we had only one bed and it remained that way for several years, even after my sister Rosalyn was born. I remember that a large trunk was put beside the bed and we had to sleep crosswise with our parents' feet resting on the trunk. My grandmother had her own bed, and Uncle Jim slept upstairs when he was home. He was away a good deal of the time, living in Riverton or Gimli or some camp while he was fishing. Later as we got older, we, too, could sleep upstairs where there was a partition separating two rooms.

There was a large kitchen attached to the house. We had a wood-fired cook stove, and a homemade table and chairs. My mother made curtains to cover the cupboards, which held the dishes and pots and pans. There was a cellar where the perishable foods were kept. In the fall, the house would be made ready for the winter. It would be "mudded," which meant that mud was plastered between the logs. Then it was lime-washed to look nice. Banks of earth would be put around the base of the house. All this preparation helped keep the house warm in winter. The fires went out during the night and it could get very cold. Early in the morning, my uncle or dad would get up and make a fire so that by the time we got up it was not as frigid. Still, we stood near the pot-bellied stove as we got dressed for the day. There were times when we burned our behinds when we got too close to the stove to put our socks on. There was no electricity at the time and light was provided first by coal oil lamps that later gave way to Aladdin lamps and gas lanterns, which gave a better light.

Dad was away from home a lot, fishing, hunting, and trapping, so as the oldest child I had to do various outdoor chores. He would leave plenty of wood split and ready for me to carry into the porch where it was stored. I hauled the water, and in winter this meant using a chisel to make a hole in the ice big enough to fit a dipper in to scoop the water into a pail. For bath night, usually Saturday, I had to haul enough water or snow to fill the aluminum washtub. The youngest was the first to get bathed, then the next youngest, with a bit more hot water added for each person.

During these early years of my life, I never felt that we were poor. We had a roof over our heads and never went hungry. We lived off the land, so to speak—my father fished, hunted, and trapped. We always had fish, deer, or moose meat. He also trapped beaver and muskrats, mainly for the pelts. I remember eating roasted muskrat, but for some reason we never cooked beaver. He also snared rabbits, so we had plenty of rabbit stew and soup. My mother canned as much fish and meat as was available. Suckers, a kind of fish for which there was no commercial market, tasted delicious when canned and made into fish patties. In the summer and fall we picked berries with my mother. This was a fun time, as we would pick berries with my aunts and their children. There was a little competition, as my mother would say, "OK, pick berries fast and don't be eating them. Don't you know that Auntie Annie already has twenty-six quarts put away?" We picked strawberries, raspberries, moss berries, cranberries, plums, crab apples, and even hazelnuts that we would keep in a bag to dry until Christmas. Year-round we had preserves for dessert. We would buy mainly lard, sugar, baking powder, bologna, garlic sausage, and salt pork from the one general store on the reserve.

I was thirteen years old when we moved out of my Uncle Jim's house. Dad had built a lumber house with brick siding on the site of his old house, which then became a warehouse. We were all very proud of our new house, and on moving day, I remember, as we were bringing our belongings, we would say, "Which room?" as if it were a mansion. It was actually a rather small house with three bedrooms, a washroom with only a wash basin, with no bathtub or toilet, as there was no running water, and, of course, a living room and a kitchen. It was new, and we were very excited about it. I had helped my dad shingle the roof. Having a hand in it made me all the prouder.

ELEMENTARY AND HIGH SCHOOL

It was not until I was ready to go to high school that being a non-Status Indian mattered. In those days, around 1950, most of the children from Fisher River were going to the Birtle Indian Residential School after completing grade eight. I was ineligible because I did not have status. In retrospect, I see this as a mixed blessing. The two teachers at our school were aware of my situation and offered to have me take grade nine by correspondence. Miss Lewarne was the teacher of the senior grades and was prepared to coach me. She had grades three to eight to teach besides helping me. As it turned out, I covered very little of my grade nine program. Instead, I helped her with the other grades. I may well have been the first teacher's aide in a reserve school.

Unbeknownst to me, Miss Lewarne and Miss McGill, the Junior Room teacher, worked through that year to find a school for me to go to the following fall. They approached the Women's Missionary Society of Canada (WMS) to sponsor me to go to the town of Teulon, which was about 160 kilometres south of Fisher River. The WMS would cover my board and room at twenty-five dollars a month and the tuition. I lived in the Girls' Residence that could accommodate fifteen girls. We attended Teulon Collegiate. The girls were mainly from rural farming communities that did not have high schools in those days. They were Ukrainian, German, Swedish, and English, and then there was me, the lone Native. This was the first time I had been away from home and my first experience with non-Natives other than the teachers who came to teach at Fisher River. I found it strange and lonely at first, but not for long, as I soon enjoyed the friendship of the other girls who, I was to learn, were not much different from me.

There was a comparable Boys' Residence with the same backgrounds as the girls. One day, one of the boys called me "Pocahontas." I felt this was a racial slur! It was the only time while in Teulon that I noted anything that might be construed as racism. When I tell this story, I say, "Had I known that Pocahontas was an Indian princess, I may have taken it as a compliment." It may well have been a compliment, as the boy who called me Pocahontas became my boyfriend. I got on well, and during the second year in Teulon, I was on the eight-member student council as a sports convener. I organized recess and noon-hour sports such as volleyball and softball, as well as weekend sports that in winter were monopolized by curling. Being on the student council gave me two years' experience in not only organizing, but in public speaking, as I had to give oral reports at our assemblies.

It was in the fall of 1951 that I entered grade ten at Teulon Collegiate. I had always done well in school on the reserve but grade ten was difficult. One reason was that I did not have a solid grade nine and also because I found it very exciting to go home with my girlfriends on weekends. Those who came from the nearby towns such as Inwood, Komarno, Lundar, and Petersfield got to go home for weekends. I found their families were very kind to me. My friend Alice's brother taught me to drive on an old Model T. They had cattle, and every day Ed would go out to the field in the Model T and set the dogs free to round up the cattle. It was in this field on a farm near Inwood that I got my first driving lesson and plenty of practice, as it was one of my favourite weekend haunts. What I really enjoyed were all the country dances that were held in these towns. We loved going to Crabby Steve's Barn, a dance hall in the Komarno area. It was not unusual for us to go dancing on both Friday and Saturday nights. I had a great time, but my schoolwork suffered.

While at the residence we had two-hour study periods each school night, and not much got done on the weekends. At the end of the year I found myself "short a few courses"—in other words, I failed some courses. In those days, it was possible to write supplemental examinations in August. I did this, but it cost me a summer of fun. My Uncle Jim no longer lived in the house he lived in when I was younger. His house was now next door to our new house. Since he was out fishing, his house became my place to study. I would spend time studying whenever I could since I realized that I really needed to pass those subjects. I cannot recall what they were but I do know one was health. Imagine that! I passed chemistry, but failed health.

Every year, before all the high school students were to return to school, the community put on a farewell dance. This year it was held at Mike Crate's, just a few houses from where we lived. I could hear the great music coming from the open-air dance hall. I loved to dance so much, but I knew that I might not pass my exam if I was out late, so I tried to study. The next morning, the man who was to drive me to Fisher Branch, a town about fifty-five kilometres away where I was to write the exam, did not show up. I had to go looking for him since he was the only person with a car on our reserve. I finally located him and we were off to Fisher Branch. He had been at the dance and recounted how much fun it was. Well, I arrived an hour late, but due to the circumstances, I was allowed to write the exam. Thankfully, I passed, though by a slim margin. With this result, and passing another exam a few days earlier, I would be allowed to go on to grade eleven still carrying grade ten math.

This did not deter my enthusiasm for school. I wanted to go back for grade eleven. I asked my parents what they thought I should do. My mother always took the upper hand when it came to decision making. She suggested that it might be better for me to "go out in the lake"—this was a common expression meaning that I should go to work at a fish camp. In my case, the only job I might be able to do was to be a "cookie." Being a cookie meant that I would help the main cook with duties such as peeling potatoes and preparing other vegetables for cooking, as well as washing dishes, setting tables, and so on. Usually these were short-term jobs during fishing season. This did not appeal to me at all because, first of all, I really did not know how to cook and I did not care to learn. Being the eldest in the family, my primary job around the home growing up was to do the outdoor chores such as carrying water from the river, carrying wood, and emptying the slop pail. My sister Mary Ann was the one who helped in the kitchen. It was 1952, and fishing was not good, therefore money was scarce. It did touch me when my mother told me years later that she cried many times when she wrote to me and could not even put a dollar in the envelope for me. It did mean a lot to get a bit of money while at school. I know her suggestion to go to work was based on the hard times they were facing and not because education was not important to her. When she was in her fifties she took upgrading to grade ten. I asked her what she was going to do with her new credentials and she said, "When I was young I couldn't go beyond grade eight and I want to get at least grade ten."

In many cases, it is not our parents who encourage us to go to school. It can be someone totally outside the family. For me, one of these people was Betsy Flett. She was around my mother's age and whenever I would see her, usually at the store during holidays, she would ask me about school and say, "Good girl, keep on going to school." Another person was Mrs. Stattin, whose husband owned the general store at Fisher River. She was very interested in my education and encouraged me to go on. Long after my high school years, she kept a scrapbook of clippings that would occasionally appear about me in the newspaper.

My Uncle Jim was my main source of help. He would send me money now and again, and I remember among other things that he paid for my lovely yellow graduation gown. One time, I wrote to him and asked him if he could send me some fisherman socks, as I needed heavy socks when I went curling. One day, I received a parcel and very excitedly opened it in front of some of the girls only to find stinky socks with holes in them. Of course, he was playing a joke on me but it did cause me some embarrassment. New socks came shortly thereafter.

I was able to get a weekend job at the local bakery that doubled as a bus depot. My job in the bakery was to wrap the bread. You put the waxed wrapper around the bread, folded the sides and sealed them with some gadget that heated the ends enough to hold them together. I did get to serve the customers at the lunch counter now and again. It was the place where the bus to and from Hodgson made its stop for refreshments. Residents of Fisher River would go to Hodgson, a distance of thirty-eight kilometres, to catch the bus to Winnipeg. I got to see people I knew quite often and at least got to say hello to familiar faces. It seems strange now, but it took me a while to know the difference between a sundae, a banana split, and a float. The job paid me fifty cents an hour.

The summer after grade eleven, I got a job as a clerk at Pezak's general store in Dallas, a small settlement about twelve kilometres from Fisher River. I sold the usual general store items but I also had to buy Seneca root dug by people from Peguis and Fisher River. This meant carefully weighing the root and figuring out what it was worth. During that time, I lived with John Pezak's mother. She would serve me eggs for breakfast, eggs for lunch, and eggs for supper. Was I tired of eggs! Fortunately, I did not work all through the summer, as I wanted to go to United College to pick up my math course. My sister Ida, who lived just a few blocks from the college, let me stay with her. The few dollars I earned helped pay my tuition for the three-week intensive course. I was delighted to pass my math with a mark of 75 percent. Thanks to Miss Mills, who was a fabulous math teacher, even I could get through it all. I was reading an autobiography of a colleague who also credits Miss Mills for getting him through math. There were probably hundreds of students who were able to continue their education, thanks to Miss Mills.

Though my high school grades were not impressive, I did manage to get through. I graduated in 1954. My mother, dad, and little brother Reggie came to my graduation. It was a momentous occasion for my family. I did enjoy my high school years, though it is interesting to note that in my twelve years of school, the First Peoples of Canada did not even deserve a mention. Fortunately that has changed over the years.

I believe it was fortuitous and a mixed blessing that I was labelled a non-Status Indian, ineligible to go to a residential school. When I hear the stories about the unpleasant, often horrific experiences of those who went to residential school, I know that I would have been one of the push-outs who dared to speak her mind, which was not tolerated in those schools. I was forced to take an alternate route for my education, and thanks to two wonderful teachers who saw some potential in me, I found a way to continue my education.

CHAPTER TWO

My Teaching Career

REEDY CREEK AND BELLHAMPTON

After grade twelve, I was among a number of Teulon Collegiate graduates who attended a six-week summer school for permit teachers held at the Manitoba Normal School located in Winnipeg. It was 1954, and there was a serious shortage of teachers. Those with grade eleven or twelve were readily recruited for teaching jobs. Off to the Manitoba Normal School we went for a crash course on teaching methods, and a review of English and math and other subjects. The summer school program did not present any great challenges. We learned how to balance attendance registers, as well as the basics of classroom management. I was eighteen years old. Being a teacher had been my childhood dream and it was quickly coming true. I am not sure who helped cover my tuition for this program, but I suspect it was my Uncle Jim. My parents had little money to spare and they had my siblings to feed and clothe.

After finishing the course, my friend Jane Ann, a fellow Teulon graduate, and I applied to Bernard Grafton, Supervisor of Special Schools with the Manitoba Department of Education, for jobs in what was known as "underdeveloped areas" of the province. These schools usually had multiple grades and were located in isolated areas that did not attract qualified teachers. We did not mind. We just wanted jobs. My salary for that first year was $1,600, and we were paid over a ten-month period. After deductions, the pay was $152 a month. I was assigned to teach at Patterson School in the Métis settlement of Reedy Creek. Jane Ann got a school ten kilometres from me in another Métis community, Kinosota. I had thirty children in grades one to eight, which was not unusual back then.

We arrived at night and we were taken to our respective boarding places. I was to board at the home of Charlie and Isabel Tanner, very close to the school. I was given a room and would eat my meals with the family. Ray, their six-year-old son, would be starting school for the first time that year. I can still remember the feeling I had that first morning of school. We had been told that we must begin the day with the singing of "O Canada" and repeating the Lord's Prayer and to end the day with the singing of "God Save the Queen." I had written out the words to all of these as I was afraid that I would not remember them in my nervousness. Here I was, at eighteen years of age, facing an eager group of thirty children ranging in age from six to fifteen. There were seven children from one family—that meant one in just about every grade. The oldest child in this family was fifteen, just three years younger than me. He was a mature young man who helped keep his siblings in tow, as did many of the other older children. I believe I was blessed with this placement, as I had a great year. I had been given one bit of extremely good advice by one of my former teachers. She said, "Be strict with the children at the outset so that they know that you mean business and won't tolerate fooling around." That sound piece of advice put me in good stead throughout my teaching career.

Yes, I had a good year, but just how much did I teach them? With eight grades, you assign work to each grade and the period is almost over. You might manage to work with one class per period. I believe that in those one-room schools, the children learned much on their own and learned from listening to the teacher instructing another grade. Despite the challenges, I like to think that I created a climate of learning for them. The parents were very accepting of me. While I knew that they were mainly Métis people, not much was said about their identity. They must have known that I was Native, as they included me in the life of the community. I was often invited to evening meals in their homes. As for teaching, at that time no one heard much about culture and I taught the curriculum with no thought of including anything about Métis culture. Times have changed a lot. Today, the people of Reedy Creek and Kinosota readily embrace their Métis identity.

I had an interesting social life that year. I was a fun-loving young woman. Jane Ann and I found ourselves in communities with ever so many great-looking young men. This was the era of country dances, and most every weekend we would be at dances in our communities or other small towns, such as Alonsa or Amaranth. The dancing was mainly waltzes, polkas, fox trots, and schottisches. With all these young men to dance with, there was a lot of fun. Both Jane Ann and I went steady with a few of these fellows for what was likely a few weeks at the time. I got more serious near the end of the year and had one steady boyfriend to whom I became engaged during Christmas of 1955.

I intended to save enough money to attend the provincial normal school to get my teacher's certificate. With my meagre salary as a permit teacher I could not save enough money that first year to put myself through a year of normal school, so I opted for another year of teaching. I did not make this decision until sometime later in the summer. I contacted Mr. Grafton again and told him I would like a teaching job. He was very happy to hear from me and offered to drive me to the community he planned to assign to me. The job at my previous school had already been taken and I was assigned to Bellhampton School, in a Ukrainian farming community about twenty kilometres north-west of Amaranth. This time I had ten students to start with, and to my great surprise one of them, aged fifteen, got married during the Christmas break. It was much easier to work with ten than thirty children, and I basically provided individualized instruction, though I did not know that is what it was called at the time.

That year I boarded with a Ukrainian farming family. For the first time in my life I put on some weight, as I had plenty of cream and all those pork and beef products, as they kept cattle and pigs, as well as doing some grain farming. When I was growing up on the reserve, my mother would be concerned about how skinny I was. She would encourage me to eat, saying, "You're so skinny, people will think we don't feed you."

The school was three kilometres from where I was boarding. I went to school by horse and buggy in the summer and horse and toboggan in the winter. The family I boarded with had two sons in school—one was ten years old and the other was seven. The older boy would hitch up the horse and we would be off on our three-kilometre drive to school. One winter day both boys were sick and I had to drive the horse to school by myself. I had never driven a horse before. The landlord told me not to hold the reins tightly but to let the horse find the way. Sure enough, the old horse got me there and one of the older boys took the horse to the barn and hitched it up for me again at the end of the day.

My cousin Doreen taught in Amaranth, so I spent most weekends with her. My social life was still one of going to dances and house parties. My boyfriend worked in Winnipeg and was able to return most weekends. There was one occasion when we had a huge snowstorm and the roads were blocked almost everywhere. I missed a whole week of school because there was no way for me to get back, as our road remained blocked. Finally, at the end of the week, a man from the community came for me with a horse and sleigh that had a seat in it. It was still storming and he had brought bricks that were heated up to keep my feet warm. I was glad to get back to my teaching. It was the one and only time that I missed a block of days in all my years of work. I have been blessed with good health.

I did not go out during the week, as there was really nowhere to go. All there was in the community was a school and a Catholic church. Most people went to Amaranth to shop. My landlord and I got in the habit of playing cribbage after supper. I enjoyed the game, and would say that I played well. My father had taught me how to play at a young age. He taught me how to count quickly so I learned to recognize hands at a glance. My landlord was a good player so we were evenly matched. At some point we started playing for a penny a point, and we kept track of this carefully. As luck would have it, I ended the year with enough points that I did not have to pay for my board and room for the month of June. I saved myself thirty dollars.

These two years of teaching were a positive experience for me, and I knew then that teaching was, indeed, my destiny. As I reflect on being in high school at Teulon with town and farm kids of many backgrounds and cultures, I realize that I simply followed the trend and headed to a teaching job, as did a number of my classmates. Would this have happened if I had been in a residential school? It is doubtful.

Working for a second year as a permit teacher proved no more successful than the first year in terms of saving money. My raise was $100, and I was now making a salary of $1,700 a year. At the end of that year I saw that it was futile to think I would save enough for a year at normal school. Then I learned about student loans from the government. In the fall of 1956, armed with a student loan, I entered normal school full-time.

GOING TO NORMAL SCHOOL

By then I had expanded my circle of friends interested in teaching. Beverly Olds, whom I met at summer school, was from Warren, Manitoba. We became life-long friends. What I remember most about my non-Native friends is that for them, like me, money was a challenge and we were all from rural areas and unfamiliar with the city. Bev had taught for three years on a permit. We considered ourselves somewhat knowledgeable about teaching and felt we could assess what was really important when it came to the courses being taught. At least, that is what we thought.

Bev and I were able to room together. There was accommodation in the main building and in the huts. These were temporary war-time structures that became residences for the students. We were fortunate to get an end unit in one of the huts that was larger than most rooms. We shared the room with a young lady from the Russell area. Being an end room, it had an exit to be used for fire emergencies. It came in handy for us when we stayed out beyond the curfew and had to sneak in. There were rules about leaving the campus. We were required to sign out and to state where we were going and when we were expecting to return. I cannot remember what the punishment was for disobeying rules. Fortunately, we were never caught. It was a long way downtown from the normal school in Tuxedo. We did not have cars, so we would walk one kilometre to Assiniboine Park and take the streetcar from there. I think the fare was ten cents. We had an uncanny principal, Mr. Lightly, who amazed us by always remembering our names, though there were nearly 500 students. Our classes went from Monday to Friday and from 9:00 a.m. to 4:00 p.m., much the same as a regular school day. The classes consisted primarily of courses that we would be teaching in elementary schools. The focus was on methods courses, how to make lesson plans in various subjects, and how to maintain discipline and keep our registers of attendance. There were no courses that taught us how to work with multiculturalism. The assumption was that "one size fits all."

During our year of teacher training we were required to do two weeks of practice teaching in a city school and two weeks in a rural area. In the city, I went to Norquay School in the inner city, where there were quite a number of Indian children. I chose to teach about the great horned owl to a grade one class for my teaching assignment, which would be supervised by one of the normal school faculty members. The stuffed owl that I took to class did get the attention of the children.

I went to Fisher River for my rural placement. The instructor came to spend a day at Fisher River observing my work, at which time I was required to teach a class. I had carefully written up my lesson plan on the wind, but when my supervisor arrived I found that I had forgotten my lesson plan at home, more than a kilometre away from the school. I was very embarrassed, but was allowed the time to go get it. I guess the lesson was fine as I passed "practice teaching."

I did not find my normal school training to be much of a challenge. I did not worry about the fact that I did not have any courses that taught me how to teach on an Indian reserve, though I had planned to go back home to teach. I was just another person who decided to become a teacher and held no particular expectations of the institution.

I was now twenty-one years old and very much involved in the social scene. Elvis Presley made his debut that year. The first time he was to appear on television was on the *Ed Sullivan Show*; Bev and I went to my sister Ida's apartment to watch him on her thirteen-inch black-and-white television. It was worth it, and like most young people of the day we were loyal fans of Elvis, who happened to be the same age as me. Being in Winnipeg, we attended fewer country dances and got to city ballroom dances instead. On occasion, we dressed up formally, such as on the Sadie Hawkins night, a big event in those days, when women asked men out on a date. As the story goes, if a man rejected your offer, he would have to give you a gift, usually of your choice.

No one I know refused the offer of a date, so I don't know if that is true. The women made huge, outrageous corsages that the men were required to wear. By then, my fiancé and I had introduced Bev to his cousin, and they were dating. When she was visiting me this past summer, we laughed as we passed the Cambridge Hotel on Pembina Highway, remembering the number of times we sat outside the hotel while our boyfriends were in the pub having a couple of beers. Women were not allowed in pubs or any drinking establishment at that time. After their few beers, we were off to our function. There was a place called the Monterey Dance Gardens, out near Headingley. At this establishment, patrons could bring in their own booze, but it had to be placed under the table. I don't think this was legal, but it was done. Patrons could buy whatever they required as a mix for their drinks. For some reason, the fellows always brought lemon gin for the ladies. To this day, I can't stand the thought of lemon gin. On these special occasions, there were usually several of us couples out on the town together.

With graduation over and armed with our interim teaching certificates, we were ready for our teaching assignments. To become a qualified teacher with a first-class permanent teaching certificate, you had to have one year of normal school and three six-week summer school programs.

During the latter course of the summer, superintendents from various school divisions, representatives from Indian Affairs Branch, and the Supervisor of Special Schools were at the normal school on a recruiting mission. I only went to the session held by Indian Affairs, as I had made up my mind that I wanted to teach at Fisher River. I was reminded that it was not wise to go to one's home community to teach. I know I was not told this because I was an Indian—it was standard practice to discourage all new teachers. My argument was that I had already taught for two years. At that point I had no great ambition to enter Indian education to make it better. In fact, I never thought school was substandard at Fisher River. Whatever my motivation, I just knew that I wanted to teach there. I do remember that in making my argument to Indian Affairs about going there, I said, "What do you think I went to normal school for? I want to teach my own people."

FISHER RIVER

I did wonder what the reaction of the people of Fisher River would be to having me as one of the teachers. I was the first Indian teacher from Fisher River that they would have. I was very conscious of this fact and knew that I would have to make sure I did a good job. They knew me from childhood; it was important to me to show the people that I was not going to put on airs just because I was a teacher. More importantly, I wanted to be a good teacher. What helped me the most in this regard was the fact that I was a Cree speaker. At that time many of the parents spoke mainly Cree and I made sure I spoke to them in Cree. I tried to be friendly to everyone and took part in community activities. I went to church and became the leader of the Canadian Girls in Training (CGIT) and taught Sunday school.

Fisher River School had three classrooms. The junior-room teacher, as she was called, taught grades one and two; the intermediate teacher taught grades three to five; and the senior teacher had grades six to eight. I was the intermediate teacher. There were about twenty-five children in my class, including my sister, Darlene, and numerous cousins. I was very mindful of relatives in my class and wanted to be sure that I did not appear to favour them over the others. My sister bore the brunt of this, as I was very hard on her. She was extremely shy and seemed to lack confidence. I demanded much from her, and to her surprise she was improving immensely in her schoolwork. One time, she turned in a perfect paper on her health exam. It consisted of multiple-choice, fill in the blanks, and one open-ended question. It appeared that she should receive 100 percent but I was reluctant to give it to her, as no one else was scoring 100 percent. I asked one of the other teachers to look at the paper and I made sure that the name of the student was blocked out. When she gave it back to me, she said, "This is a perfect paper." So I gave her full marks. There was no repercussion from the students, as they had come to trust me by then.

A few of the boys in my class had been difficult to handle by their previous teachers. It soon became evident who those boys were. As had been my practice at my two previous schools and on the sound advice of a former teacher, I was determined to enforce strict discipline at the outset. This meant using the strap, if necessary. Corporal punishment was permissible in those dark days. One day, I took three boys to task for misbehaving. I got the strap out and took them into the hallway, closed the classroom door, and strapped each one on the hands. I was a five-foot-two, 110-pound teacher. My sister later told me that the boys were smiling when they entered the classroom. The next time trouble arose, I followed the same procedure, but this time I made sure that they would not enter the room smiling. I must have given a few extra on each hand, and the first boy began to cry. I then opened the classroom door and sent him in. The children saw that he was crying, and I think that cured him along with the other boys. Their reputation as being the tough boys in the class was challenged.

In retrospect I am not proud of using the strap, yet we thought nothing of doing so then. The upshot of this episode was that the boys did become better behaved. And, more importantly, they came to respect me and were able to concentrate on their schoolwork. One of those boys is now a grandpa and the father of our first lawyer from Fisher River. Years later, when he was already a married man, he still insisted on calling me Miss Kirkness. That was also a problem for my sister while I was teaching there. I did not live with my parents when I taught there, so whenever I would go home for a visit my sister would want to talk to me, and she would say, Verna, Miss Kirkness, Verna, Miss Kirkness....

It was 1958–59, my third year of teaching, when I became the principal of the three-roomed school. We were still fifteen years away from setting a policy that would enable Indian parents to be involved in their own education. Yet common sense must have prevailed, as I started parent-teacher meetings because I thought it would be a good idea to have the parents involved in the school. At our meetings, I spoke to them in Cree. We discussed school matters, and I had a "question box" for them to put in any questions they might have about the school. To be sure we talked about attendance and discipline, I would plant questions in the box. It worked, and I felt from the discussion that I knew their feelings about certain matters. After the business part was over, we would play active games to have a bit of fun. Some of the parents were real jokers, and so we had a good time. We ended the evening with sandwiches and cookies that were provided by the parents. We may well have had the first parent-teacher association on a reserve. We had excellent attendance, as grandparents and others attended as well. It may have been seen as a social function, as there was not a whole lot to do on the reserve in those days.

In addition, on given Friday afternoons I introduced a parents' visiting day. They were invited to come to the school to see their children's school work and to observe them in action. My children were great singers and we sang for the parents. As the principal, I was required to leave the classroom at times when someone came to the door on business. I often asked the children to sing Christian choruses while I was out of the room. We had quite a repertoire of songs, some requiring action. I was so pleased when I'd return to the classroom to see them singing away heartily.

Christmas concerts were a long tradition and very special occasions at Fisher River. Usually a stage would be built in one of the classrooms by the fathers, who would do it on a voluntary basis. We decorated the classroom, and each of the three classrooms contributed a number of items to the program. Drills and short plays were popular. I remember putting on a mock country-western TV show. I had an announcer and I called the station "Sookey Kanawapy," which translated from the Cree means "watch intently." I had a trio of girl singers who were known as the "Wesakachak [Cree legendary hero] Sisters" singing "Silver Bells." I managed to have all the children in my class take part. There were square dancers, and we even had Elvis Presley present singing "You Ain't Nothin' but a Hound Dog." We played a record, and the one playing Elvis was lipsynching. A toothless comedian, as was often seen on those types of shows, completed the scene. Because we used Cree and related to people and incidents on the reserve, this mock TV show was a hit and is still remembered by those who were in it.

I recall another incident that is remembered to this day by some of my students. To promote good health practices, I struck health teams. I would have a monitor for each of the five teams who would check to ensure that the children had clean fingernails, had washed properly, and brushed their teeth. On one occasion I played a trick on them and asked the children on a Monday morning how many had had a bath. The homes did not have running water except for the manse where the United Church minister's daughter lived. I knew how difficult a weekly bath was, as I had experienced this during my whole life on the reserve. On that Monday morning, I asked the children who were standing up after their routine health check, how many had had a bath over the weekend. I said, "Remain standing if you did." Two or three sat down. Then I announced that I had a lie detector and would use it to make sure everyone was telling the truth. As I walked up and down the aisles, most of the children quickly sat down before I came to them. Then I admitted that what I had in my hand was a light monitor for my camera. We all had a good laugh.

I do not recall consciously trying to make the curriculum relevant to the children's lives. However, I must have instilled pride in being Indian in some way. Perhaps it was just that I was an Indian and a teacher. I had Shirley, a ten-year-old blond Irish girl in my class. She was the daughter of the United Church minister. Apparently, one day Shirley went home and asked her dad if they had any Indian blood in their background. She said, "Think hard, Daddy!" as he explained to her that he and her mother were from Ireland and that they did not have Indian blood. I recall another incident with Shirley. It was exam time, and she asked her dad to pray for her to do well. He said, "Yes, I'll pray for all the children." Her response was, "But Daddy, if you do that, Delmar will beat me."

It was during my time at Fisher River that I decided to officially become a Kirkness. I had been known as Kirkness ever since my mother got married. I realized that I had better do this before I got married because it might cause problems, and also all of my credentials to that point were in the Kirkness name. I hired a lawyer, and we had to go through a strange procedure of having both my own mother and dad adopt me. Not only was that strange, but I found out that even my first name was not right. The records showed me as Hilda Jane Williams. I couldn't believe it. My mother said she definitely registered me as Verna. At least my middle name, Jane, was correct. On April 30, 1958, I legally became Verna Jane Kirkness. Not only was I illegitimate, but now I was adopted.

Shortly after that, I broke off my engagement. We had been planning a double wedding with my cousin Doreen and her fiancé for the upcoming summer. I had been engaged for nearly four years. We had many friends in common; I knew his family well, as he did mine. It was a disappointment and meant a drastic change in my life. While I had other meaningful relationships in my life, I believe this experience was an indication that I was destined for a different path.

I taught at Fisher River for two years. I would say that my two years teaching on the reserve were good. I regard that experience as an important milestone in my career. I had in my mind that I would develop the pattern of teaching at each school for two or three years to experience teaching in a number of communities. Not having been to residential school, I decided to ask for a transfer to the Birtle Indian Residential School, located in western Manitoba, to see what it was like.

BIRTLE INDIAN RESIDENTIAL SCHOOL

It was now the fall of 1959. With my luggage stowed away in my car, the 1951 Ford I had bought from Miss Fairservice, one of the teachers at Fisher River during my first year there, I was off to Birtle, a four-hour drive from Winnipeg. I was assigned to the grade three and four class that was housed in a building separate from the main building. There were four of us teachers covering grades one to eight. The high-school students went to the town of Birtle, just over a kilometre away. I found the children in my class just as enthusiastic as my previous classes. Two of my cousins from Fisher River, Stanley McKay and Evelyn Kirkness, were in high school there. It was nice to get to see them now and again. Joanne Sinclair from home was in my class. She and her sister were there because their grandmother who had taken care of them was no longer able to do so. It was rare for children from Fisher River to be sent to residential school before reaching high school.

The children in my class enjoyed staying after school to help clean the classroom but mainly they wanted to visit. I think they wanted personal attention since there were many of them under the care of one supervisor, a kind of surrogate parent. Many of them were very caring people, but having fifty or more children in one's care was far too many. The high-school students often dropped in for a chat. This kind of closeness was frowned upon by the school administration. Instead of being happy to have an Indian teacher in their midst with whom the children could identify, the administrators tried to discourage them from spending time with me. I did not feel welcome at the school. I would have gladly left there after a year, but pride would not allow me to do so. I did not want to give the administration the satisfaction of having forced me to leave.

The second year, I was assigned the grade-seven class. It meant that I would now be in the main building. I wondered if the principal arranged this to be better able to discourage children from spending time with me after school. I wondered if they were afraid the children would tell me things about their lives away from the classroom. The practice of shooing kids out of my room by the principal, senior teacher, and matron continued even with grade-seven kids. The students just wanted to visit and chat as children normally do. The grade-eight teacher, who was also the senior teacher, really did not want me around. She acted like a watchdog, eager to chase the children to their dormitories.

This was the first real negative school experience that impacted my life as an Indian person. I knew something about residential schools, but being there and seeing children who were away from their parents and communities, sensing their loneliness and what I perceived as unfair treatment, made me uneasy. During a history class, I was suddenly aware of the inaccuracies of history. The authorized history textbook for the course was called *Canada: Then and Now,* by Aileen Garland, who had been one of my normal school social studies teachers. I sensed the facelessness of our ancestors. Yet they had taught the newcomers to this land how to survive and to travel the vast and harsh waters and terrain. The only acknowledgement in the book would be a reference to a nameless Indian guide. I pointed this out to my class and very soon found out that they, too, felt this omission. After talking more about it, I asked them to write an essay entitled, "Canada, 1959, Without White-man." Well, the response to this assignment was overwhelming! They wrote pages and pages about what they thought it would be like to live in Canada without the influence of people from other lands. I wish I had kept some of those essays, as they revealed so much about the students' feelings, which were probably enhanced by their confinement to an institution. Unfortunately, this epiphany did not have a lasting effect as I continued to teach just what the curriculum dictated.

As was typical in the residential schools of the day, the boys and girls were segregated to a ridiculous degree. Even brothers and sisters regardless of age did not get to spend time together. They had an outdoor skating rink near the school, and even then if a teenage couple were skating together for more than a couple of minutes, they would soon be told to break it up. The senior teacher from her convenient spot indoors from which she could observe the rink would call on the loudspeaker, "OK, Joe and Evie, break it up." They were high-school students who eventually married. Both are now retired and living in Fisher River.

On Thursday evenings, I taught the senior high-school boys how to dance in my outdoor classroom. It would have been easier to teach them to waltz, polka, and schottische if they had female partners, but that was not allowed. Enid, one of the girls' supervisors, and I took turns dancing with the boys to the music on a record player. More often, we all danced up and down the classroom in a row as they learned the steps. It was fun all the same, and the boys actually did learn to dance. When I met the boys long after they left school, they would talk about my Arthur Murray dance lessons.

All the students in the school, from the youngest to the oldest, had chores to do. While for the young ones it was dusting the stairs or cleaning sinks, for the older girls it meant working in the kitchen helping with meals; the older boys helped with the farm, milking cows, and cleaning the barn. On one occasion, one of my students had just finished her work in the kitchen and was on her way up to her dormitory. She met the principal as she was running up the stairs. She was startled and dropped the cookies she had been carrying in her apron. Well, taking food from the kitchen was a no-no, and she was in trouble. Humiliation was one of the main forms of punishment. She was taken to the auditorium where the children were watching a movie. The movie was interrupted as the principal proceeded to reprimand my student in front of the children. The student became furious, and as she told me, lifted her arm in a motion to take a swipe at him while he berated her. She was a big girl and could have packed quite a wallop. The next morning I was told the details of this incident. By now, I was getting fed up with what was happening.

After that incident I took it upon myself to contact the Women's Missionary Society, which was in charge of the non-teaching staff at the residential school, to complain about the treatment of the children. As a result, a woman was sent to the school to spend a week talking to the children and the staff and generally observing what was going on. It was a week like none other, as the staff, in general, were perfectly behaved and the principal, in particular, was the most charming person one could wish to have working with the Indian children. I saw him one day skipping down the hall with a couple of the little grade one girls on each hand. Skipping down the halls certainly would not have been tolerated under ordinary circumstances. It was a good week for the children, as they did not suffer any humiliation under the watchful eye of the visitor. However, nothing ever came of the visit that I am aware of, and as far as I could see life was back to normal as soon as she left.

For each of the two years I was in Birtle, I volunteered to escort the children from the Hudson Bay line to their respective home areas. This meant a train ride of two days and one night to arrive in Churchill, the end of the line. The cook at the school had packed a large box of sandwiches and fruit for us to eat on the way. I was in charge of ensuring the children ate, slept, and got off at the right stop. Sleeping was a challenge since they had to sleep on the seats. Some of the main stops along the way were at Ilford, Gillam, Thompson, and Picwitonei. Some children lived between these communities, in places referred to as Mile 247 or Mile 418, for example, where there was no community. Getting off at the right stop was something of a nightmare as I had to let some kids off the train in the middle of the night. All I knew was that Peter and Sarah were to be let off at Mile 350. I would check with the conductors and they would be very good at letting me know when the next stop was coming up. Off would go the children, and I had no way of knowing if someone was there to meet them because the train would immediately be on its way. When fall arrived and the children returned I would feel relieved to see Peter and Sarah appear.

Birtle Residential School was reputed to be much superior to the Brandon Residential School. Students from Fisher River were normally sent to Brandon, but once they learned about Birtle, most chose to go there. One good thing I can say about Birtle is that the children were very well fed. The staff ate exactly the same food as the children, except for having a separate dining room. On Sunday evenings, it would be like having Christmas dinner. The school had a huge farm, and they slaughtered their own cattle and hogs and had their own milking cows. They had chickens and turkeys. The older boys did much of the maintaining of the farm. I might say that at Birtle they fed the body, but deprived the soul of the children.

After two years teaching at Birtle, I decided to move on and I applied for a transfer to the Rossville Residential and Day School in Norway House. I felt that I needed to experience another residential school to see if Birtle was typical or not. My assessment of Birtle was that had I been a high-school student there, I surely would not have been able to tolerate the regimen, or the repressive and confining atmosphere, and either would have dropped out, as many did, or would have been expelled for breaking one or more of the many rules.

I was in Birtle from 1959 to 1961. I had now completed six years of teaching. I enjoyed teaching and got along very well with my students. I followed my rule to start out very strict so the children would know that I meant business and would not tolerate fooling around. Then, once that was established, I could let up and enjoy the class. It worked for the students as well; they were comfortable and happy in my classroom and could relate to me with ease. I think they identified with me because I was an Indian too. It certainly was not because I was teaching them from a Native perspective. I was just teaching as I had been taught to do and followed the Manitoba curriculum using the authorized textbooks—none of which had anything to do with Indians.

Instinctively, I must have known that I should be doing something different. I noted that the children did not have trouble mastering the curriculum as laid out, but I do feel that it did nothing for their self-esteem when there was little or nothing in their studies that related to their own lives. That may have been the reason why I enrolled in a six-week summer course on cross-cultural education offered by the normal school. I was even more enthusiastic when I learned the course was being taught by a Native American professor. It would be the first course I would take in cross-cultural education and the first course taught by a Native person. I was the only Indian teacher in the course. I became friends with Dorothy Fahner, who was in the cross-cultural course, and was happy to know that she was going to Norway House to teach since that was my next destination.

ROSSVILLE INDIAN RESIDENTIAL AND DAY SCHOOL IN NORWAY HOUSE

On the day of our departure to Norway House, Dorothy and I met at the airport, all decked out in our high heels and short, tight skirts. We were in style! Well, to our surprise, we were to be flying in a Canso plane, which could land on the ground or on water. It did not have a normal door entry; instead, you entered through the top of the plane, which proved to be no easy feat in high heels and tight skirts. If we thought that was difficult, it was much harder getting off the plane. At Norway House, having landed in the water, we had to disembark onto a dock when the water was low. We were on the plane with other new Norway House teachers, and we all laughed about this experience when we got better acquainted. It is hard to imagine that, having been raised at Fisher River, I would not know better than to dress so inappropriately for a trip to a northern reserve. I had only had one plane ride previous to this, and it was from Thompson to Winnipeg. The plane was small, but you did walk on through a door.

I was assigned the grade three class. My love for teaching continued. There were around 300 students, half of whom lived in the residence, with the other half coming from the community. There were twelve classrooms for grades one to eight. The principal was Mr. Lee, a married man with four young boys (one other was born later). In the residential schools, those in charge of the residences were called principals, though they were not educators. The person who headed the academic unit was referred to as the senior teacher.

At Christmas of that first year, I was approached to become the assistant senior teacher because the person holding that position was not able to continue due to poor health. Keith Johnson was the senior teacher and had been there for a number of years so I felt confident that I could work with him and would get good direction. The position was to assist in making orders for supplies, doing the monthly reports, and taking on other duties the senior teacher assigned. These I did during noon hour or after school. At the end of the year Keith had decided to leave to take up another position. I was offered the senior teacher's position. I did not want to take it, as I felt that I was achieving all that I wanted in being a teacher. I got a lot of pressure to take the job from Roy Carter, who was a regional superintendent of Indian Affairs, in charge of Rossville School. While I have often criticized Indian Affairs for unfair treatment, I have to say that Mr. Carter was determined to have me take the position. I might say he shamed me into it by saying, "You owe it to your people." I had never felt any obligation to my people, though I was compelled to work among them. All I wanted was to continue to be a teacher. I did accept the job, and it changed the course of my life. I was now in charge! I not only had myself to consider, but a slate of teachers and 300 children.

As the senior teacher, I taught grades seven and eight on a half-time basis. My other time I spent on administrative duties. Mr. Calver and I shared the class, and his additional duty was to teach industrial arts. We introduced kindergarten to the school, assigning the job to Dorothy Fahner. During the first few months of the school year she and I walked to the various homes in the community to discuss the new kindergarten program and to encourage the parents to sign up their children. Word was getting around that Dorothy and I were looking for five-year-olds. When we walked in to the Hudson's Bay store, the parents would pretend to hide their little ones from us as a joke. The kindergarten got off to a good start and Dorothy, having had early childhood training, was an excellent teacher.

We also started an arts and music festival. This was something that was very popular in Birtle, as teachers trained their students in choral work, singing solos, choir singing, and doing folk dances. They would compete with children from all over the district. The Birtle Residential School children, from grades one to twelve, won many awards. The students at Rossville School benefited from the introduction of the festival. I remember my class of grade sevens and eights memorizing a long poem called "The Forest Fire." Many of my students were fifteen to seventeen years old because many started school late. They took part willingly and their voices in choral work were rich and lovely. We had three teachers on staff that could play the piano and could read music. They each taught a number of students who showed an interest in music, introducing some classical pieces to their repertoires. The arts and music festivals continued for a number of years.

I held parent-teacher meetings (as I had in Fisher River) with the parents of the day-school students. It was even more important here that the meetings be conducted in the Cree language, as it was very much the language of day-to-day communication. In fact, children often entered school knowing only Cree. This presented a challenge, and at this point we did not entertain the idea of teaching in the Cree language. It probably would not have been acceptable to Indian Affairs, as the "English only" policy was in force. Still, we did not punish children or even discourage them from speaking their language, nor was this enforced as part of the residential school. We did have a Basic Oral English program designed by Rose Colliou, who was hired by the Department of Indian Affairs as a consultant. It provided much needed assistance to the teachers and followed a repetitive approach where conversations were designed for everyday speech.

I loved Norway House, this community where my grandfather and his parents lived for a time. The area known as Rossville is where the residential school was located along with a Hudson's Bay store, the United Church, and many homes. The area where the old Hudson's Bay fort was built was simply known as the Fort. It had a Bay store, Royal Canadian Mounted Police headquarters, and the hospital. We liked to go to the store at the Fort on Saturday mornings even though we had a store in Rossville. At that time you could get from Rossville to the Fort only by boat in summer and by Ski-Doo or Bombardier in winter. For an outing in the winter, we often walked (in our mukluks) the six kilometres across the ice. There were no cars, no highways, just trails for snowmobiles, Bombardiers, horses, and people. Soon after we arrived at Rossville, Dorothy and I, along with two men, one a teacher, the other the school chef, bought a sixteen-foot aluminum boat with an eighteen-horsepower motor that cost us $650. As soon as school was out on Fridays, we would head up the river for an evening of fishing. I can still hear the singing of the frogs as we sat by our campfires in the evening.

The social life of teachers, nurses, RCMP, and other outsiders at Norway House were the weekend parties where far too much alcohol was consumed. The parties were sometimes in the Fort area, or at Forestry Island, another part of Norway House, or at other company headquarters. During the summer, we travelled by boat to these destinations, often with inexperienced boatmen who had been drinking. The danger didn't really occur to us then. There were a number of romantic relationships, with competition between the female teachers and nurses for the RCMP officers. Many met their mates at Norway House and married.

We did not have television and radio reception was very poor. Our contact with the outside world was snail mail or two-way radio telephone. During freeze-up and break-up we didn't get mail for one to two months. Two-way radio was not an easy way to communicate. One incident that is often spoken of when my friends remember the Norway House days is the conversation between one of our male teachers and his sweetheart, whom he left behind in Winnipeg. Feeling very lonely, he apparently decided to propose to her. After connecting with the radio operator, the normal procedure was to say "over" when you wanted a response from the other party. On the days when reception was poor, the operator relayed the message for you. So the fellow calls his sweetheart: "Hello Jenny, this is Mark. Over." "Hi Mark, good to hear from you, but I can't hear you very well. Over." "I'm calling to ask you to marry me. Over." "You want me to do what? Over." "I want to know if you will marry me. Over." "Sorry, I can't make out what you are saying. Over." The operator cuts in and relays the message: "He wants to know if you will marry him. Over." "Yes, yes! Over," she says. The radio operator relays that message back. The funny part of all this is that everyone who has a two-way radio in the north can listen in to the conversation, but Mark was new to the area and not yet aware of that. The proposal was reported all over the north about the heartsick teacher at Rossville School.

There was a record player in the common room on the third floor of the residential school. It was also the floor on which most of the single female staff lived. The male staff had rooms on the top floor of the annex that had classrooms on its main floor. We got together in the common room and played cribbage or other card games and listened to singers such as Peter, Paul, and Mary, Johnny Horton, and even Odetta on long-playing records. My friend, Dorothy, was good at sewing and knitting. She made me a beautiful silk dress for a special occasion and made one out of velvet for herself. I am not one for knitting, but I decided to join some of the others who spent time knitting, crocheting, or doing embroidery work. I tried to knit a nice red pullover for myself with a little help from my friends. Well, the fellows decided they wanted to try their hand at knitting too, so it became a staff project. The outcome of that was not good. In the end, I took our very poor effort to my mother at Fisher River, who saw that it was not salvageable and ripped it out and made some socks instead.

A number of us were curlers and we decided to prepare a sheet of ice for curling. It was just outside the school and had rings at only one end. We used jam pails for rocks until Dorothy was able to get curling rocks donated from the curling club in Gladstone. We made do with that until Dudley Jones, an employee of Indian Affairs, suggested that we build a curling rink. A committee was formed to oversee the building, and all who were interested agreed to put in $200 for the building supplies. We made a rink that could hold two sheets of ice. We all pitched in to build it, and the women were not spared from hammering nails and sawing boards just like the men. When it was ready, we got several of the local young people involved in our curling teams. Upon leaving the community, the committee was able to reimburse the $200 to each contributor. The rink remained for several years.

The teachers usually went south for the Christmas break. We had quite an experience one time when a group of us decided that rather than go by plane we would hire a Bombardier to take us to Grand Rapids and be met there by a station wagon for the trip on to Winnipeg. This was intended to be a cost-saving measure. The evening before our departure we had attended a Christmas party that went quite late and a fair amount of beer was consumed. The next morning we set out with Mr. Richardson, the United Church minister, as our driver. We had been given a lunch to take along by the kitchen staff. As our departure was early in the morning, we did not have time for breakfast. Soon after we started off, we dug into the sandwiches and cookies. About halfway to Grand Rapids, Mr. Richardson stopped to refuel. He had a drum of gasoline on a trailer that we were towing. Well, lo and behold, there was no gas in the drum, as it had leaked out as we travelled along. What were we to do? Fortunately, a short while later another Bombardier came along on its way to Grand Rapids, and they were able to share their gasoline with us. This was a chance in a million, since few people travelled this route. When we were about fifteen kilometres from Grand Rapids, both Bombardiers stopped and the drivers conferred. They decided that the passengers would be let off on the shore near some trees, and they would combine the remaining gasoline and go on to Grand Rapids in one vehicle. With three men, the load being much lighter, they thought they would make it. Those of us left behind began to scour the bushes for dry firewood and made a giant fire to try to keep warm. We had no food left and it was already late afternoon. Someone shared a box of chocolates, but they didn't last long. We were getting colder and colder. I had on a Hudson's Bay three-quarter-length coat on that I burned a hole in when I had my back to the fire. We were kept busy getting firewood. My dad later told me that we should have built two fires and stayed between them to keep warm. We were all greenhorns when it came to outdoor survival. At one point we saw a plane go by and we were all waving scarves and tree branches to attract them. It just flew by. The men who had gone on were taking much longer than anticipated. It was getting dark by the time they got back to us. They had run out of gas about eight kilometres from Grand Rapids and two of them had walked the rest of the way. When they finally reached us, it took some time to get our Bombardier going, as it had been idle in the cold for a long time. Fortunately, we all survived the ordeal, but by this time it was nearing daylight. We then continued on by station wagon to Winnipeg. I got off at Ashern, where my mom and dad were to meet me the day before at about 3 p.m. I called them from a pay phone in Ashern and they came to get me, a distance of about ninety kilometres. They had been worried sick about what might have happened to us. It was a trip that we will never forget. My friend Dorothy and I still repeat the story, and her husband says it gets better every time.

Norway House was far different from Birtle. It did not feel like a prison, though there still was a girls' side and a boys' side. Yet, there was more mingling of the boys and girls. Siblings could visit one another. Mr. Lee, the principal, was a very gentle man, and his wife was the same. The teachers were wonderful, and many were involved in the community. All the children attended the United Church. Several of us teachers and other staff members taught Sunday school and sang in the choir. Dorothy was the choir leader and organist. We all took part in extracurricular activities after school. Some worked on sports (baseball, hockey, curling), one taught wood working, another had cooking classes. I had a class in good grooming for the teenage girls. There was so much going on that the children had little time to be bored. I remained at Norway House for three years. Being the senior teacher was a good experience, and having such good colleagues made a difference. In fact, during the second year I was at Rossville, three other Indian teachers were hired. That meant that the ratio of Indian to non-Indian teachers was four to twelve. I believe this would be a record for any school in the early 1960s. To this day, I continue to be in touch with a number of the teachers who were on my staff during those years. We all look upon those years very fondly.

The children could only go as far as grade eight at Rossville School. If they were to continue they went to a residential school in the south or to Teulon, where the residences had been taken over by Indian Affairs in the 1960s. Others went into private home placement in Winnipeg, a new approach of Indian Affairs. The thinking was that the students would feel less lonely if they stayed with a family. It concerned me greatly to see the number of students who were returning to the community because they were very lonely, and those in Winnipeg found it difficult to cope in a big city. I knew from observing them over the years at Rossville that they were bright kids. As I thought about it, I felt they needed someone in the city they could relate to and who would help them in their adjustment to a new home, school, and city life. I approached the Indian Affairs superintendent and told him I would be interested in going to Winnipeg to assist the students. I was not aware of counselling or that a counselling program already existed in Winnipeg and The Pas.

A pattern was beginning to take shape in my life related to any romantic liaisons. Though not consciously, I seemed to move on when things got serious. I mentioned earlier that Dorothy and I had purchased a boat and motor with a couple of fellows, one a teacher and the other the school chef. We kept close company with them during that year. In the following years, I always had a male friend. When I decided to leave Norway House, I did leave behind a fairly serious relationship. I left, and he stayed on in his teaching position. Once again, I moved on, following my instinct to help young people. I wanted the students who went to Winnipeg for high school to succeed. It was my desire to help them do just that.

CHAPTER THREE

Beyond Teaching

COUNSELLING IN WINNIPEG

When I moved to Winnipeg in 1964, most of the Native male students were in trades and vocational programs such as upholstery, carpentry, automotive and diesel mechanics, or drafting; most female students were in hairdressing, clerk typing, and practical nursing programs. The majority had been out of school for a number of years and had taken upgrading classes to qualify for further training. A growing number, however, were coming to Winnipeg for high school because of a new initiative taken by the Department of Indian Affairs to see if high school students fared better when living with families in private homes. Jack Witty, a former teacher in Indian schools, had been the lone counsellor for the students in Winnipeg. When I came on the scene, Jack and I made the logical split: I would work mainly with the girls while he would work with the boys. The counselling program was administered by the Department of Indian Affairs, so I was simply transferred from Norway House to Winnipeg and paid as a teacher.

It was a pleasure to work with Jack. He was a very caring man and did his utmost to help the students. Jack was my only source of orientation to the job. He took me around to the various schools attended by the students—Success Commercial College, Pollock's Hairdressing School, and Red River Community College.

I enjoyed working with the girls, young women, really. I did my best to encourage them to complete their courses. They faced many challenges, as some had dependents to look after—children or partners, some of whom did not have jobs. It was a painful experience when a student dropped out and all of the counselling in the world could not persuade them to continue. One young woman came in one day to tell me that she had to quit because she was pregnant. She was such a lovely person with a lot of potential that I was sad to see her go. I remember seeing her pass by our office frequently on her way to do day work, usually housework, to support herself. There were other heartbreaks along the way, but on the other hand, it was a happy time when a student completed a program. We did our best to prepare them for their job interviews, emphasizing that they should show confidence in responding to questions. Many were shy and quiet and had difficulty making positive comments about themselves because bragging is frowned upon in many Indian cultures. Despite that, they usually found employment in their field of training.

The Indian Medical Services had a strange policy when it came to dental work. Several students needed extensive work but could not receive it unless we could assure Medical Services that the student would have a job where they would be highly visible. We usually managed to make a case for the student since most were in hairdressing, clerk typing, or practical nursing programs.

We also had a lot of laughs in the office with the students as we shared stories or chuckled at some of the ways to solve a problem. Money was always an issue. I enjoyed it when one day Ethel came by with a poster she wanted me to put up. It read, "Why is there so much month left at the end of the money?" How true!

When it came to the high-school students, we had to look for suitable homes where they would board. It was referred to as the Private Home Placement Program. There were no specific criteria to follow in the selection of homes: we just had to do our best in making decisions. We tried to find homes for students near the schools they were to attend, so they were scattered throughout the city and the suburbs. We ensured that the house was adequate and that they had a decent bedroom, that the family was financially sound, and that they were kind and friendly. In the majority of cases, the placement turned out fine. Occasionally, we had to move a student for one reason or another.

Each student received a monthly bus pass and a personal allowance for incidentals like toothpaste, shampoo, haircuts, and entertainment. I knew that what they were receiving did not adequately cover their needs. We introduced the students to the YMCA and its many facilities. Some became members of young peoples' groups and community clubs, and attended functions at the Indian and Métis Friendship Centre.

With the increasing number of students coming to Winnipeg, several more counsellors were hired the next year. None of us had specific training in counselling, as there was no training available at that time. We did have one thing in common: we had all been teachers in Indian schools. By the second year there were five of us in the counselling unit, three of whom were Native.

At our monthly gatherings with the students, we took advantage of the opportunity to speak to them as a group about how to manage their money, taking their school work seriously, completing assignments on time, and so on. In order to get to know our students well we visited them in their homes during the evenings. This meant that we had very long days.

It was a difficult time for our students: the temptations of the city were hard to resist. There were many Monday mornings when we would have to go to court because one of our students was arrested by the police over the weekend. Most of these incidents had to do with drinking. I came to dread Monday mornings. There was one of two judges usually on the docket on these mornings. One judge understood the challenges faced by our students. The other was a fierce man who made not only the accused shudder but made those of us there, to help and support, feel totally useless. On one occasion, I was at court to support a hairdressing student of mine who had been arrested for drunkenness. The fierce judge was on the docket, and when my student appeared he reprimanded her. Then, as was the custom, I got up and told the judge that she had been doing very well in her hairdressing course, that I was sure that this experience would teach her a lesson, and requested that she be given a chance to prove herself. The judge's response was quick and mean: he said, "You would do better to cut her hair and make her look decent." Well, the student was usually well-groomed, but after a night in the drunk tank, what was he to expect? He did let her off. We always hoped for the understanding judge when our students had to appear.

I felt a sense of failure for every student that we lost. As I look back at all the positions I have held, I would have to say that this was the most difficult. I do believe we made a difference, though I can't say that we were able to help each student to be successful.

It was during this first year as a counsellor that I was invited to Norway House to speak at a convention attended by teachers from Cross Lake and Norway House. I was asked to speak about the counselling work we were doing in Winnipeg. I believe this was the first formal presentation I ever made to a fairly large group. It was January 1965, and I had four months' experience as a counsellor. I explained the work that Jack Witty and I were involved in as we tried to assist the students.

I spoke of the Private Home Placement Program because a number of Norway House and Cross Lake students were away at high school in Winnipeg. I explained that the rationale for private homes was for the students to enjoy a more natural home life than they would at a residential school and that the student could be part of the family rather than just a boarder. Looking back, I see that this is what we hoped for, for the students and the program. In reality, things were more complicated.

Since most of the homes were with non-Native families, our students had to get used to a different way of life in totally different cultures. Some resented the fact that they were expected to be part of the family, as they felt it meant abandoning their own families. Often on the weekends they would gravitate to the North End around Main Street, where they would likely meet up with people from their communities or at least other Native people. This is where the trouble would start, as they would get caught up with those who were drinking. On the other extreme, there were homes that worked out very well and in which students had a long-lasting relationship with their boarding families.

I went on to explain that we visited the schools and spoke to the teachers about the students' progress and attendance. Examination results were sent to our office. Business colleges and hairdressing schools send us monthly reports. After those in trades completed their training, we assisted them in finding jobs by suggesting appropriate dress for the interview and coaching them in questions to expect. I hoped to impress upon the audience that counselling covered a host of concerns related to the students' boarding homes, their families, their courses, their teachers, and their money or lack of it. Most importantly, we worked to keep their spirits up with constant encouragement. Little did I know that this was the first of many speeches I would make in the course of my career.

When I enquired about working with the students in Winnipeg while I was senior teacher at Norway House, I was sure that what was needed was an understanding ear from a person who cared about them. I found that it wasn't that simple. My fellow counsellors were great people who went above and beyond the call of duty to assist the students. There was no way we could save every one of them. Loneliness was just too much for some. For others, the temptations of the city were too accessible and they fell into one of the many traps. As mentioned earlier, there was no training or orientation for us to do the job. When my friend Pat joined our counselling unit to help me with the girls, I did brief her on what we were to do, but my main concern was "Don't let them drop out." I occasionally meet up with some of the students that I counselled. Some have done very well. In fact, one is completing her PhD in education at the University of Manitoba. Others are now retired after successful careers.

My experiences in this job were varied, interesting, and sometimes frustrating. Our superintendent of schools, who was in charge of our counselling unit, was extremely pleased with the work I was doing. He saw me taking the lead in the unit and felt that I should be promoted to become head of the unit, along with an appropriate raise. He made the request to headquarters in Ottawa, as they had to do in those days. The request was denied on the basis that I did not have a degree. While I did not request this promotion and was happy to do the work, I felt slighted at this decision. I saw it as a lack of appreciation for my efforts. What did Ottawa know about our day-to-day work?

I shared an apartment in Winnipeg with Loreen, who had been one of the teachers on my staff at Norway House. She had a teaching position in East St. Paul. We decided to have a party to which we would invite all those we knew in Winnipeg who had at one point worked at Norway House. I began to date a former teacher from Norway House who attended our party. During that winter he was taking a university course toward his Bachelor of Education. I was busy with my job, but found time to type his papers for him. For me, that was the height of devotion, since I was a "hunt-and-peck" kind of typist. It was ideal when he was hired to work as a counsellor in our unit. Then we were able to see each other frequently. It was a great time for me, but eventually our relationship began to unravel. I was now the unofficial head of the counsellors. I was a take-charge sort of person, and maybe this kind of aggressiveness on the job affected our relationship. Now I can only speculate.

Again, I retreated from the situation, this time to travel to Asia with my friend Pat. I knew Pat from my Norway House days, as she was my assistant senior teacher for a year. She had moved on to teach in Winnipeg. During the time I was working in the Indian Affairs regional office in counselling, I recommended that she be hired as a counsellor. She had made a previous trip to Singapore to visit a childhood friend who had married a British officer and were posted to Singapore. We decided to take a month during our summer vacation to travel throughout Asia. All our fellow counsellors were at the airport to see us off. I knew that my relationship was going downhill and this trip was a welcome diversion for me.

Our first stop was in Hawaii, where we stayed at a Waikiki Beach hotel. Even though our plane arrived late at night, we were up bright and early the next morning to walk on the beach, which was still deserted. From Hawaii, we went to Taiwan. To our surprise, we had a private car with a driver and chauffeur to take us around Taipei, the capital city. We had a prepaid tour so we did not know what to expect. The sights and sounds were all very interesting. Then we were off to Tokyo, Japan. Pat said that she needed a bathing cap. We found a department store and went to look around. I wandered around with Pat in plain view. A few minutes later, she approached me and said, "Don't you ever do that again; you look like everybody here." I laughed and said I had no trouble knowing where she was and that I was not lost. It was the first of many experiences where I would be mistaken for an Asian person. At restaurants, they would speak to me in their language, thinking I was one of them. I did not respond, but Pat would say, "She doesn't speak

Japanese!" We visited other parts of Japan—including Kyoto and Nagasaki. We bought Japanese kimonos and I looked right at home in mine. There is definitely something to my notion that my biological father was Asian.

From Japan, we headed for Bangkok, Thailand. This was a magnificent city with all the pagodas and a canal streaming with boats and business. We had a guide who was with us throughout this time. He took a shine to Pat and was very attentive. We decided to get out of the city for the weekend and booked a cabin at a lake. We were asked if we wanted one with a fence or not, and we opted for the one with the fence for privacy. Well, when we got there the fence was about a foot and a half high. We laughed because we probably paid more for this cabin than if we had had one without a fence. Another incident in Thailand was when Pat and I went to have our hair done. She has naturally curly hair and required only a shampoo and blow dry. I, on the other hand, had straight hair requiring rollers that took much longer to attend to than Pat's. When we went to pay, Pat paid the equivalent of $2.50 Canadian, whereas mine cost me fifty cents. My Asian look was a decided advantage. When we went to a dinner show, we were asked if we wanted anything to drink. For some reason, we were very thirsty and decided to have a beer, not our usual choice. The waiter asked us if we each wanted one, to which we answered somewhat indignantly, "Of course." To our surprise, we each got a litre of beer. Needless to say, we did not finish our drinks.

Our next stop was Hong Kong—a fascinating place, especially for shopping. There was competition from various vendors who expected us to bargain with them. I enjoyed bargaining and had a great time. Three-piece wool suits were in fashion at the time, and I found that I could order a tailor-made suit that would be shipped to Canada. I bought two suits for twenty dollars each and paid with a personal cheque. I was not sure I would ever see the suits, but they arrived a few weeks after I returned to Winnipeg. They were a delightful and lasting part of my wardrobe. Pat saw a string of Chinese lanterns that were ideal for putting on a Christmas tree. They were fragile and she had to take special care to get them home in one piece. When she were plugged them in, they blew up (because the wiring was different). The irony of this story is that after we got home she found that they were available in local stores.

Our final destination was Singapore, where we stayed with Pat's friend Lulu, her husband Dick, and their three children. Lulu had an *amah*, a servant who cleaned and did laundry for them. Their *amah* had become very close to the family and was pleased to help in whatever way she could. While we were there she did not want to take her days off, as she feared that Lulu would not be able to take care of us. Lulu certainly enjoyed this service and joked that she dreaded Thursdays, because this was the day she had to make her grocery shopping list. I remember the *amah* inviting us to her place for a meal. She lived in a modest, small home and cooked some of her traditional food for us. Lulu and her family did not treat her as a servant, but as a friend. It was very hot, as it was late July and we were only kilometres from the equator. It was not uncommon to have more than one shower a day to cool off. We would barely have our clothes off and the *amah* would have them laundered by hand and hung to dry. One day, Pat and I were going shopping and required pedicab transportation to get there. Lulu advised us how much each segment would cost and said that I should handle the payment, as they would think I was one of them and not ask for more if they thought we were tourists. We did as we were told and, sure enough, we got by just fine. We were quite proud of ourselves when Lulu took us to the Raffles Hotel that first made Singapore Slings, which are famous all over the world.

On our way back, the plane stopped in Manila in the Philippines for refuelling, and we were able to get off the plane. As I entered the airport a little girl came running up to me calling, "Auntie, auntie!" It was an eventful trip, and my acceptance as an Asian person most fascinating.

Sometime in 1965, I met Jim Wright, who was a counsellor at one of the residential schools. We had had a counsellors' conference where I was the guest speaker. In later years, he spoke of being very impressed with me, and that on the first night he met me we had gone around the world together. A group of us got together one evening for a progressive dinner. We went to a Polynesian restaurant for drinks and appetizers, to an Italian restaurant for dinner, and finally to a German one for dessert. As it turned out, from that time in 1965, we have been a part of each other's lives. In 2005, we had a private celebration to mark the forty years that we have known each other.

Jim came unencumbered: like me, he had never married and was deeply interested in Native education. He was actually the ideal mate for me.

I had a unique experience during my time as a counsellor. I was asked to chaperone Rosalie Kirkness, a thirteen-year-old Cree girl from God's Lake Narrows (550 kilometres north of Winnipeg) to Expo '67 in Montreal. With our surnames being the same, people assumed she was my daughter. This experience for Rosalie began when she wrote a letter to the American Iron and Metal Company requesting films and pamphlets for a class project. Her letter was referred back to Canada to the Canadian steel industry. This so impressed the officials of the company that they decided to invite this young girl from an Indian reserve in northern Manitoba, rather than a VIP, to open their pavilion.

I met Rosalie at the Winnipeg International Airport. It was her first plane ride and first car ride. She seemed excited, though she did not say much until she spotted a dog riding in a car. She thought this was hilarious, as dogs were only kept as sled dogs in God's Lake. I had been given her whole itinerary. We were to go to the Hudson's Bay Store where a store fashion designer had been assigned to help her select a wardrobe for her trip. Among the selection was a green miniskirt and leotards. Photographers were there taking pictures of her in her various outfits. She had certainly never had such an experience at God's Lake. In Winnipeg, she visited the legislative building and met Sid Spivak, the Minister of Industry and Commerce. He presented her with a tartan tam and she gave him a beaded centennial crest.

We flew to Montreal. When we arrived, photographers were waiting for her. They asked her to get back on the plane to have a picture taken with the captain and stewardess. We were escorted to the Holiday Inn in a limousine. Rosalie was so excited about everything, and so she should have been—this was an experience of a lifetime for anyone, including me. We were treated like royalty. During every spare moment, Rosalie watched television, another first for her. Our days were full of interviews with the press, sightseeing, and room service. She loved to eat. Her favourites were french fries and desserts. She always wanted dessert for breakfast, but I would not allow it. Before the grand opening, we were taken to visit the company's steel plant in Hamilton and treated to a visit to Niagara Falls. As we were approaching Niagara Falls,

Rosalie was greeted on the radio. She was a celebrity! We had a lovely suite in a hotel in Montreal.

On the opening day of Expo '67 we were escorted to get our first view of the site. Rosalie was to cut the ribbon to open the Steel Pavilion. I had coached her in how she was expected to carry out this task. She was as gracious as a princess with her white gloves on. Well-groomed for the occasion, she was the delight of the many people who were there. She cut the steel ribbon with a large pair of scissors and thus officially opened the pavilion. She made the headlines in the newspapers. It was a wonderful experience for both of us.

There was a downside to this experience, though. Since Rosalie had never been away from her reserve in northern Manitoba, she had no idea about what life was like beyond God's Lake Narrows. She was under the impression that the experience we were having was how people outside of God's Lake lived all the time. She was not excited about going home. She wanted to stay with me in Winnipeg. I kept in touch with her while I was in Winnipeg, but lost touch when I left.

I was not seriously planning to leave Indian Affairs until I saw an advertisement in the *Winnipeg Free Press*. Frontier School Division #48 was advertising for a supervisor of schools. I had met the superintendent, Mr. Ken Jasper, at a conference in Yellowknife where I was a keynote speaker. I phoned him and told him I had seen the advertisement and wondered if I should apply for the job. We chatted a bit and got around to the fact that I did not have a degree, though I had twelve years of work experience and I was Native. He did not tell me to apply and we left it at that. Later that day, he called me and said, "If you want the job, it's yours." I almost collapsed and I wasted no time in telling him I would take it. In September 1967, I was at my new office in Dauphin, Manitoba.

SUPERVISOR OF SCHOOLS

Frontier School Division #48 was formed in the 1960s by the Manitoba Government to serve rural and northern communities in Manitoba, many of which had a Métis population. Several northern Indian Affairs schools also joined Frontier School Division. In all, about 200 teachers were in the employ of the new division. I was hired as a schools' supervisor; it was my job to supervise the 200 teachers. My superiors were an official trustee, Mr. Ken Jasper, and his assistant, Mr. Abe Bergen. There were also two support staff. We were housed in the courthouse in Dauphin. My office was the judges' change room, which was a very small space. When the spring and fall court assizes were held, I had to move out to make room for the judge. His robe always hung on the hook at the back of the door.

My job was much like that of a school inspector: my responsibilities were to evaluate teachers by observing them, checking the students' schoolwork, and checking enrolments and attendance. I have often remarked that, had I been a man, I would very likely have been called superintendent. In fact, in later years this position was called superintendent. As a supervisor, I visited the schools and observed the teachers in action. I looked over the resources that were in each classroom, checked the teachers' daily plan books, and some students' workbooks and notebooks. My main concern was with the effectiveness of the teachers and ultimately whether and how the children were learning.

The schools varied in size, with some, like Grand Rapids, having as many as twelve classrooms and some one-room schools, like the two in Norway House on either side of the reserve, referred to as North and South schools. In those days, the province and the federal government sometimes had schools in the same community. The enrolments ranged anywhere from seven children to more than 200. With 200 school days in a year and 200 teachers to supervise, I was very seldom in the office. I did some serious driving and flying during my three years at Frontier. Winter driving was a challenge, especially on roads that were not well-travelled. There was stretch of about 200 kilometres from Gypsumville to Grand Rapids with nothing in between, which in the winter could pose quite a challenge. We were required to carry winter gear, such as sleeping bags that were good for fifty below zero, warm parkas, and some food. I always carried baker's chocolate, some nuts, and crackers. Fortunately I never had to use my emergency supplies. I do remember a spring trip when I saw a black bear just up the highway on the way to Grand Rapids. I thought it was neat. So I got my camera and from several yards away I took a photo of the bear. When I told my dad about seeing the bear and taking its picture, he scolded me for doing that and pointed out how dangerous it was. I guess I was fortunate that he was a friendly bear.

There were communities that I had to fly into and back then you flew in Canso, Cessna, Beaver, or Norseman planes that had different capacities for passengers or freight. They landed in the water on pontoons or on skis in the winter. I flew in a one-passenger plane one time on my way from Selkirk to Berens River. The plane was slow and could easily be affected by a headwind. On one of my trips, a bush plane belonging to another company caught up with us, flew past us, then came back to fly side by side with us, with the pilot waving at us to go faster, before taking off at its regular speed, at least twice as fast as we were going. Bush pilots really had a sense of humour and knew one another. I guess it helped them endure the harsh and dangerous conditions they faced every day. When I stayed for more than one day in the communities with larger schools, I usually stayed with the principal and his family or one of the teachers. This was rather uncomfortable after spending the day evaluating the work of teachers and principals.

There I was, a thirty-two-year-old Cree woman with no education beyond normal school, supervising teachers and principals, several of whom had degrees. I loved teaching and think I had a good sense of what a good teacher should be like. I had always loved school and modelled myself after the teachers that I liked when I was a student. Of course, having been a principal at Fisher River and Norway House provided some experience supervising teachers. That year, along with this very demanding job, I had started taking a university course by correspondence. I was on the road or in the air early Monday morning or sometimes even Sunday afternoon, and was lucky if I returned home by Friday night. Then I had my course to work on over the weekend. It was a demanding time, physically, mentally, and emotionally.

Frontier School Division covered 288,000 square kilometres, the largest geographical school division in Manitoba. The schools were miles apart, and I did manage to visit each school at least once. I ended up doing a lot of troubleshooting. Of course, I spent more time where I felt teachers were under-performing. I tried to work with those teachers. One of their main problems was discipline. We had much less tolerance in those days with children making noise in the classroom. I still don't believe that children can learn if they do not listen to what the teacher or fellow students are saying. I found in several schools that the children were absolutely unruly and the teacher was unable to bring any order to the classroom. During that first year, I convinced a few teachers that they should seek other employment. I did not fire them, which was a good thing, as I may have had a lawsuit on my hands. I was not aware of the provincial rules regarding employment and that I would be expected to provide extensive documentation on a teacher before consideration would be given for his/her release. However, I did not see this job as just looking for trouble spots. I think it was great for those good teachers to have someone who could recognize and acknowledge the work they were doing. I observed many good teachers, but like everything in life it is the problems that get the attention.

Principals and teachers are always wary of any kind of outside authority. I had to be diplomatic in my dealings, especially with the principals, most of whom were male. I always met with them first and talked over generalities regarding the school and sought their guidance as to problems I should be aware of, including the physical condition of the school. I clearly remember one case where I had spent a few days at one of the larger schools that I regarded as one of the better schools. I thought I had completed my visit to the satisfaction of the principal, since prior to leaving I had met with him to discuss my evaluation of the school, which was also my practice. I went to the office the next morning to find that the principal had called in a complaint to my immediate superior, Abe Bergen, about my visit. Abe and I discussed the matter. I can't recall the nature of the complaint, but Abe thought it would be a good idea if he visited the principal. I opposed his suggestion and told him if he expected me to do my job, he would have to let me handle it. So back I went to see the principal, about a three-hour drive away. I believe he was quite surprised to see me and not the big boss. We discussed his call and complaint. Nothing further came of it and subsequent visits went well. I felt that the principal resented me because he was not comfortable with a woman supervising him. It is strange, but I never felt this in any way had to do with the fact that I was a Native or that I did not possess a university education. Actually, I do not think that many people were aware of my educational status.

Two additional supervisors were hired by Frontier School Division the following year. That eased my load considerably, as now I had about sixty-five teachers and principals to oversee and the physical area was divided into three. There were times when two or three of us visited the same school at the same time, so it was not a rigid division. Working together in the bigger schools enabled us to compare findings.

Frontier had one residential high school in Cranberry Portage. They turned an old army base into this school for northern students, many of whom were Métis. It housed around 200 and had a staff that included administrators, teachers, and support staff. Most of the schools in Frontier School Division only went up to grade eight. This was a wonderful opportunity for Métis children to finally have the opportunity to complete high school. As supervisors we did not have a formal role in Frontier Collegiate, as it came to be known. However, because I am Native, the administration thought it would be a good idea for me to visit the students in the school and talk to them about the importance of education. At a recent luncheon in Winnipeg celebrating role models, Laara Fitznor mentioned that she had been a student at my presentation at Frontier Collegiate around 1968 and was in awe of the fact that here was a Native woman "who had made it," so to speak. She said I was her role model from that time on. Laara, herself a successful Métis woman, has a PhD from the Ontario Institute for Studies in Education (OISIE) in Toronto and is now an associate professor in the Faculty of Education at the University of Manitoba.

Just recently, I had the privilege of meeting the now famous Tomson Highway, who was a writer-in-residence at the University of Manitoba and an alumnus of the university. He is now nearing sixty, a successful pianist, author, and playwright known internationally. Originally from Brochet, Manitoba, and a residential school product, he has done a lot to raise the consciousness of all people about Aboriginal people. He acknowledged me at the gathering, saying that I was one of the early pioneers in the field of Aboriginal education that paved the way for others to follow.

It is interesting to note that Frontier Collegiate has not had any of the adverse publicity that the residential schools that were run by the federal Department of Indian Affairs has had. In fact, Frontier Collegiate is still in existence today and is continuing to be an invaluable asset for Métis students.

While I was with Frontier School Division, trying to be of assistance in providing a meaningful education for northern students, most of whom were of Native ancestry, I became aware of a number of problems. First, there were several schools that had too many students for one teacher to handle. I was aware that Indian Affairs schools did have teacher aides to assist the teachers in their work. As I mentioned earlier, there were two one-room schools in Norway House to serve the non-Native and Métis students. I found the South school had about forty students. I decided to ask Mr. Bergen if we could hire a teacher's aide for that school. In those days, the only quick communication with the south was by two-way radio. Because I considered this a serious situation that I wanted to resolve while I was at Norway House, I dealt with the request by two-way radio phone. As it turned out, this was a good approach because, once again, everyone in the north who had a radio could hear the conversation—I knew it and so did the administrator at the other end of the conversation. I received approval and hired a young Cree woman with a partial high school education. From then on it became a common practice to hire teacher aides in the division. The aides were expected to be in the classrooms assisting the children who had limited English or had problems in reading, math, or other areas.

From my Indian Affairs experience, I was aware that they had training for teachers' aides every summer; I had been a resource person for a number of these sessions. I have to share a funny story related to the idea of hiring paraprofessionals to assist teachers. I remember being involved in a great debate with Indian Affairs personnel about what they should be called. Should they be teacher assistants, paraprofessionals, or what? To lighten the discussion, I suggested that they be called "Band-Aides." Fortunately, that caused a laugh as was intended. They did come to be known as teachers' aides. I find it ironic that it took other school divisions years to follow this practice and now many provincial school divisions have adopted the practice of hiring teachers' aides.

Summer after summer, the Indian Affairs teachers' aides spent four to six weeks learning basic teaching techniques, many related to helping children with learning English and math. A number of experts would be brought in to present methods of learning. It was quite rigorous training. Usually these summer schools were organized by the Language Arts Specialists who worked for Indian Affairs. At Frontier School Division, where we now had a number of aides, it was evident that we needed to provide training too. I organized the first session to be held in Pelican Rapids, a Métis community with a fairly large school population. The aides were housed in a hotel at Barrows Junction, the nearest accommodations, so they had to travel an hour on a winding road each morning and late afternoon.

At some point the Indian Affairs Language Arts Specialists and I talked about these long, arduous summer sessions that gave our aides no further credentials or increase in pay. In our discussion, we struck upon the idea of working toward having a teacher education program that would be accredited. Through our initiative, Indian Affairs and Frontier School Division approached Brandon University, and the Program for the Education of Native Teachers (PENT) was established in 1969. The program ran for eight weeks each summer in June and July, leaving August as a holiday month for the aides. This meant that the aides were not in the classroom for the month of June. At the time, teachers were required to have two years of training to get a teaching certificate. By being in class for eight weeks a year, it would take five years for them to get a teaching certificate. Skeptics said that it would never work, as the aides would not go for that long. That has long ago been proven to be wrong. PENT still operates to this day, and hundreds have completed the program, many having gone on to complete Bachelor of Education degrees and others have even gone on to complete master's degrees.

I have always believed that PENT was an excellent approach to teacher education because it combines theory and practice like no other program. Many teacher education programs came into being across the country in various universities in the late '60s and early '70s. PENT is the only model I know where the student teachers (aides) are in the classroom for nine months. Programs such as PENT follow the standard curriculum of the university, though over the years efforts have been made toward providing courses relevant to teaching Native children.

The second problem I was concerned about as supervisor was the lack of Native teachers. I addressed this problem by providing teachers' aides and subsequent training for them. I firmly believed, and still do, that having Native teachers from the local community in the classroom provides a more stable teaching force because the non-Native teachers who came to northern isolated communities tended to stay for only a year or two. The second advantage to having Native teachers was that they could provide role models for the children. Seeing their mothers, aunts, or sisters working in the classrooms would show that they could do the same. Unfortunately, men did not seek these positions, as other forms of work such as fishing, trapping, and logging were available to them. The only Native teacher I saw as I was growing up was a woman from Norway House, Frances Apetagon (Campbell), who came to our reserve with her boyfriend. She wasn't even actually a teacher yet; she was at normal school. I saw her as a teacher and hung around her and her boyfriend. Her boyfriend had to give me some money to go buy something at Stattin's store to get rid of me. I followed her career for a long time and involved her in my work in the area of curriculum years later. She was my role model.

My third concern was the lack of resources pertaining to Native people for use by teachers. If Native children were expected to do well in school, I believed then, as I do now, that we must build on their foundation, not beside it. The resources typically found in schools were foreign to our children. This has been the case ever since formal education was introduced to us. The reader being used at the time for grade three was *Streets and Roads*, and it was mostly about streets, cities, huge houses made of brick or lumber with a mom who wore a white apron, a dad with a suit, and little children decked out in clothes not found in many of our communities. When speaking of this problem, I referred to it as "teaching Native kids a foreign language using foreign materials." How did we expect them to learn? I remember as a teacher how difficult it was to explain an elevator to children who had never been to a city and seen apartment buildings. The story in the reader was about a monkey who got caught in an elevator all alone and began pressing buttons that took him from floor to floor, making it impossible to catch him.

Frontier School Division was under provincial jurisdiction and expected to follow the provincial curriculum. I saw nothing wrong with the curriculum, but the textbooks and the materials were the problem. I tried to provide examples to teachers about how they could use more appropriate materials. In 1968, two little books by Vi Cowel had come out. They were called *Normie's Moose Hunt* and *Normie's Goose Hunt*. I wanted to see what the reaction of the children would be to these books. I would get small groups of children together to read them the books and show them the pictures. Because of their familiarity with moose hunting and goose hunting, they loved the stories. Unfortunately, few books of this type were available. I explained to teachers that if they were teaching geography, they should begin by talking about the rivers and lakes in or near their area before talking about the Mississippi River or Lake Superior. I was trying to impress upon them the need "to go from the known to the unknown." This was a challenge. Good teachers know instinctively, but others need the resources right in front of them, and even then find it difficult to relate to a different world.

I enjoyed the challenge of working in Frontier School Division. My superiors, Ken Jasper and Abe Bergen, were decent, hard-working men who were sincere in their efforts to provide a good education system in the north. However, like many of the teachers, they were not products of the north, so their knowledge of the north and their knowledge of Native life in the communities were limited. They were supportive of my efforts to make education more relevant. Having an additional two supervisors in my second year made the job somewhat easier. Again, as products of the south with limited northern experience, they did not initiate changes in resources to reflect the population we were working with but worked from the premise of providing a quality education as you would find in the south.

Frontier was run by the superintendent and his assistant along with an advisory board, which they appointed. The board was made up of people from the communities in the division who met two or three times a year. I suggested that each school have an advisory committee so that there would be more community involvement. There was resistance to this suggestion, and I'm not sure that has ever changed.

Frontier has now been operating for over forty years. It looks much different from its beginnings in the 1960s. The division is now divided into five areas, each with a school superintendent. They have many Native teachers in the system. There are more relevant resources available to them. Many of the graduates from Frontier Collegiate are attending post-secondary institutions and becoming involved in many professions such as doctors, lawyers, and professors. They have had at the helm of the division a Métis gentleman with a master's degree, Gordon Shead. The division has come a long way in serving the people of the north.

During the course of my work with Frontier School Division, I met Bruce Sealey, a Métis working as a consultant in special education with the Department of Education. We found we were kindred spirits when it came to Native education. He had been a teacher in Shamattawa for a few years. The first time I heard him speak at a Native teachers' convention, I remember him telling a story about trying to get a radio for his school. Shamattawa was an Indian Affairs school, so he prepared a requisition for a radio that he submitted to the Winnipeg office. From there the request had to go to Ottawa, to the Indian Affairs headquarters. After several months, he received an electric radio. He had asked for a battery-operated radio, as there was no power at Shamattawa. His next move, to requisition 400 miles of extension cord, passed the Winnipeg scrutiny, he reported laughingly. Anyone who has experienced northern teaching could relate to that story. Another story comes to mind about requisitioning. One young teacher related her story about the frustration she experienced when trying to get a water pail as she had to get her water from the lake. It would have been easier for her to buy the water pail at the Hudson's Bay store, but that was not the policy. It had to be requisitioned through the proper channels. Anyway, her pail finally arrived near the end of the school year.

Bruce Sealey became a good friend and colleague. One day he suggested to me that we write a supplement in social studies for Native education in grades one to three. I was interested in this project, and the only way we could get it done was to use our Easter vacation to work on it. We reviewed the current curriculum and transformed it to relate to Native children and their communities. Part of our introduction read: "Because most Indian and Metis children must, of economic necessity, enter the mainstream of Canadian life, the adapted curriculum attempts to make the regular social studies program more meaningful to the child. In addition, there is built into the curriculum elements of Indian and Metis history and culture to give the child knowledge of his background in relationship to himself and the Euro-Canadian community." We identified the following objectives for the curriculum:

1. To assist the child of Indian ancestry to learn in a more meaningful fashion of the contribution to man's progress of Indian individuals and groups from prehistoric to modern times.

2. To assist the child of Indian ancestry to more clearly see his role in relation to the dominant culture.

3. To assist the child of Indian ancestry to develop an appreciation of his history and culture.

(Social Studies Supplement Grades 1, 2, and 3, Department of Education, Manitoba, 1972.)

We suggested in the supplement that log houses, which were common at that time, be displayed in the supplement. It was more relevant than the split-level houses being featured. I remember speaking at a teachers' conference on the supplement, where I suggested, as I had done with other teachers I had visited in the division, that lessons on rivers and lakes should begin with the local waterways. The example I gave was that if you were teaching at Norway House, it would make sense to refer to the Jack River and Playgreen Lake. Strange as this may sound, I later observed a social studies lesson in a school not remotely close to Norway House where the teacher began by talking about the Jack River and Playgreen Lake as a starting-off point. How can you win?

In 1972, the Department of Education distributed our social studies supplement to every provincial school. We requested that copies be sent to the federal Indian Affairs schools as well. I believe this was one of the first attempts made by a Department of Education in Canada to provide relevant curriculum for Native children. This would never have been possible without the influence of Bruce Sealey, who was well regarded in education circles. It was exciting to work with him.

It was this association with Bruce that led me to my next job. The director of the Department of Curriculum and Instruction had approved our work on the social studies supplement. Over time, Bruce's work as a special education consultant had evolved to include his interest in Native education. In 1970, he joined the Faculty of Education at the University of Manitoba. He recommended to the provincial director of Curriculum and Instruction that I be hired as a cross-cultural education consultant. That is how I came to leave Frontier School Division in 1970. It was a natural progression for me, because I felt something had to be done to provide resources to teachers in areas where there was a predominance of Native children.

In the summer of that first year in Dauphin, Jim invited me to go with him on a trip to Texas. He had bought a trailer and would be using it for the first time on a long trip. We both had the summer off, as I was working with schools and he was a counsellor. I was taking a university course and had to prepare for my exam while I was away. It was a fun trip. We did a lot of our own cooking. I remember the first night on our way there we could not find a trailer park, so we parked under a Texaco sign where a garage once stood. I remember us being lost in Dallas and ending up in a Black neighbourhood. We were asking directions and were not given much help, as we seemed to be seen as intruders. It was not easy to manoeuvre that trailer around a city that was unfamiliar. We spent New Year's in a town in Texas. We bought tickets for the New Year's party that would include a dinner served around eight o'clock, followed by dancing and a breakfast after midnight. We were invited by some folks to join their group. As it turned out, they were a group of doctors and their wives. We had a wonderful time with them, with plenty of champagne and other libations. It was a good thing that breakfast was provided, because it gave us an opportunity to counteract the effects of the evening. The trailer park we were in was not too far away. It was a memorable New Year's celebration for us. We ventured further south in Texas and stayed at a trailer court in Brownsville near the Mexican border for a couple of weeks. We often crossed the border to Matamoros in Mexico to have a look in the shops, and since Jim did not like bartering I did the buying. We saw a couple of brass candlesticks that we both liked, and while they started at a much higher price, I bargained them down to ten dollars for both of them. Jim still has those candleholders to this day. In the evenings, we often went to Matamoros to nightclubs to have dinner and to dance. Our favourite song to which we liked to waltz was, "I left my heart in San Francisco" that was sung as "I left my heart in Matamoros." I did my best to get in some study time. After we returned, Jim changed jobs and became a district school superintendent for Indian Affairs for western Manitoba. This meant that he was very busy with a lot of travelling. My job entailed the same kind of schedule. We managed to get together when we could.

CROSS-CULTURAL EDUCATION CONSULTANT

I was never interviewed for the position of Cross-Cultural Education Consultant for the Manitoba Department of Education; it was more like an appointment. In fact, I was not in a competition for the position of supervisor of Frontier School Division or guidance counsellor for Indian Affairs either. To date, I had gone from being a teacher to being a principal-teacher, to counselling, to supervising teachers, and now to developing curriculum in my role as a cross-cultural education consultant. Certainly my experience as a teacher and school supervisor prepared me for the need to provide relevant programming for our Native population.

The Department of Indian Affairs had a strict policy that we were to adhere to the provincial curriculum. I was aware that the curriculum guides put out by the Manitoba Department of Education were just that, guides. However, we were expected not to deviate from the curriculum guides and to use the recommended resources. Another bone of contention for me was the "English only" policy. At that time many children were entering school knowing only their Native language. I welcomed the opportunity to address these critical issues at the source.

It was the practice within the Department of Education for consultants to work with committees in their areas of interest. For example, the social studies and language arts consultants each had committees to work with them. I was happy to have the opportunity to involve teachers from Native communities. Having worked for both Frontier School Division and Indian Affairs, I had a wide resource base. I had two priorities to begin with; both close to my heart. One was to address the language issue. How could the Native children be spending several years in school learning in a language they did not understand? I had heard at a conference I attended that in the Philippines they had a similar situation in which the children entered school knowing only their native tongue. As English was the language of commerce and business, they were required to learn English. They had designed a "language-shift" program that had remarkable results. In short, the children began their first years in school using their native language. Over the course of four years, the language was shifted to English. It seemed an appropriate method to adopt for a pilot project.

I visited a number of communities that I felt would benefit from the project, known as the Manitoba Native Bilingual Program (formerly known as the Native Language Pilot Project). I invited the teachers and parents to attend a meeting. I explained the difficulty the children were having upon entering school when they did not know English. Of course, they were not unaware of the problem. Children just sat in classrooms until they picked up enough English to learn. Since the Native language was the dominant language of the home and playground, the only time they had to use English was in school. There was no such method as Teaching English as a Second Language (TESL) used at that time, and there were no teachers in the northern communities that had specializations. I remember having a very enthusiastic response from teachers and parents at Cross Lake. Emma Jane Crate, a qualified teacher and member of the Cross Lake band, was particularly enthusiastic about the project and saw its potential. There were a number of Native teachers' aides in the school as well. I conducted the meetings in Cree. I think they tended to trust me because I was also a Native and a Cree speaker. I visited other communities—Nelson House, Oxford House, and St. Theresa Point, Wasagamack, all of which were under Indian Affairs jurisdiction. They all agreed to participate in the pilot project. Since the proposed pilot project was initiated by the Department of Education, it was not opposed by Indian Affairs. Finally, I was able to address this language issue in federal Indian Affairs schools. Among the other schools visited were those under Frontier School Division, Pelican Rapids, Berens River, a community that opted to leave Indian Affairs and go with Frontier when Frontier was established. All together, six schools agreed to participate in the pilot project.

I struck a committee to assist me with the language project. The committee members would come to Winnipeg for periodic meetings, and we worked diligently to get the project underway. We had to identify Cree speakers who could work with the children, a number of whom were teachers' aides already working in the school. The first year, we started with the nursery (four-year-olds), with a plan to add kindergarten the following year and grade one the next and so on to the end of grade three. The first year, instruction would be totally in the Native language. The teachers translated nursery rhymes and songs into Cree and Ojibway. In kindergarten, we would begin to introduce English, and more English would be added each year as the children became more comfortable in it. Once the teachers were in place and we had a plan for them to be part of PENT to get their teaching certificate, we had the onerous task of preparing materials for the pilot program. The teachers not only had to teach, but they were the ones who had to prepare materials. Initially, there was no extra remuneration for this; fortunately, they were dedicated to the cause. The committee members also assisted in preparing materials. We put together a series of about sixteen books in the Cree language for the grade-one level, thinking that these readers would be sufficient for the year, only to find that the students read them all in a short time. We had a great debate about whether to use syllabics or Roman orthography, but we opted for the latter, as we thought the transition to English would be easier than if we used syllabics. We found that not all the sounds in Cree could be found in English, so we had to improvise. In retrospect, it may have been wiser to go with syllabics to be more accurate and to introduce them to the children at an early age.

The Manitoba Native Bilingual Program was at times stymied over the years, especially when a new principal who was not familiar with the project was hired in a school. I tried to tell Indian Affairs and Frontier School Division that it was important that these principals be made aware of the language project when hired. In cases where the principals still believed that "English only" was how the children should be taught, parents became confused and I would have to deal with these situations. What I tried to impress upon parents was the fact that starting the children in school in their own language would ease their transition into English. The theory is that when we abort a child's Native language, s/he does not develop in his or her Native language, making grasping a second language more difficult. We requested that Indian Affairs provide support for this project in their schools, and they did to a point. A budget for materials and preparation time for the teachers was provided. However, I don't think Indian Affairs was ever comfortable with the concept, which was contrary to their "English only" policy. For Indian Affairs, the greatest problem was that they did not have anyone on their staff who spoke the Native language to be able to monitor it. Cross Lake stands out as a school that took the project the farthest and the longest. They carried on for eleven years until such time as Indian Affairs decided to cut off all funding.

In 1975, after four years of the program, we had an evaluation done. Norway House, a school that never had the pilot project, was our control school. The results showed that at the end of grade three the children in the pilot schools were as proficient in English as the control group. What was more significant was that, as we expected, the self-concept—how the children felt about themselves—of the children in the pilot schools surpassed that of the control group.

Over the years, new Native educators being concerned about Native language loss have talked about teaching in the Native languages. Many are not aware of the program introduced in 1970.

In 2000, I was at a meeting in Opaskwayak, after I had written a book, *Aboriginal Languages: My Talks and Papers*. In the book I had written about all my experiences with Aboriginal languages throughout the years. At this book launch, when I spoke of the Manitoba Native Bilingual Program, a man spoke up and told us that he was from Cross Lake and that he had been a student there during the eleven years of the program. He spoke of the importance of the program and how fortunate he was to be a part of it. Now as an adult he was fluent in his language and in English as well. Had the program continued and grown, it is possible that we would not be facing the crisis we are in today with the loss of our languages among our young people. At that meeting, I proposed that we launch a project called, "Cree Vision 20-20," suggesting that we could in twenty years revive much of our Cree language. The Maori had accomplished much in twenty years to revive their language. Unfortunately, the follow-up meeting we had proposed to discuss this subject further did not happen.

My second priority as a cross-cultural consultant was social studies. Bruce Sealey and I had begun the work by preparing a social studies supplement for grades one to three. Now was the opportunity to review the curriculum for other grades right up to grade twelve. I struck another committee that included teachers both Native and non-Native from the city as well as from the north. Again we attempted to parallel the existing curriculum. Our units included: the Indians of Peru (grade four), a sample study of Indians and Métis at The Pas (grade five), a sample study of Cree and Saulteaux of Manitoba (grade six), the Mayans (grade seven), contributions of Indians to World Civilization (grade eight), and a systematic study of history of North American Indians in each year from grade nine to twelve.

I had other interests that I planned to pursue in the Curriculum Branch, but as it turned out, my stay with the department was cut short because of an offer to join the Manitoba Indian Brotherhood (MIB) as its education director.

TOP TO BOTTOM

My maternal grandmother Mary Ann (in dark dress) with her sister Nancy and their grandchildren. I'm the one on Nancy's lap. We are in the yard where we lived with my grandmother. The old building behind us is the old school building that later became a Band Council House. You can see the school and the church in the background, c. 1937. (Courtesy Pat Beyer)

In the classroom at Fisher River School. I'm the second one of the s standing (age 8 or 9).

Fisher River School. I attended 1941–51. eturned to teach at the ne school in 1957–59.

A typical log house at
Fisher River, c. 1945. It
was used as a community
hall for New Year's feasts,
movies, children's socials.
It once housed the senior
grades. (Courtesy Julia
Spence)

The large boat pictured
here was used to transport
families to fishing camps
in September, c. 1945.
In front is a yawl with
outboard motor, a type
of boat used by most
fishermen from Fisher
River. Prior to this, skiffs
with oars were used.
(Courtesy Julia Spence)

Senior students at
Fisher River showing off
four crafts from Home
Economics and Industrial
Arts projects, c. 1948. I'm
the middle one in
the front.

My roommate Bev and I
studying on the lawn at
normal school, 1957.

erna and Doreen (with
fur coats), teachers at
her River School, with
mothers, 1958.

sher River. My grade 3,
4, 5 class, 1958.

My second class at
Bellhampton School,
955–56, nine children.

My grade 7 class, Birtle
Indian Residential
School, 1960–61.

My grade 3 class at
Norway House, 1961–
1962.

CHAPTER FOUR

Working Provincially and Nationally

MANITOBA INDIAN BROTHERHOOD

In 1971, a very important development was taking place in Manitoba and the Indian chiefs had decided that they no longer wanted the Department of Indian Affairs making decisions for them. The Manitoba Indian Brotherhood, the organization representing all the Indian bands in Manitoba, set out to write a position paper on what the chiefs wanted in education, health, community development, social development based on the treaties as interpreted by the chiefs. In September 1971 I was asked to take charge of the education section of this important movement. I was in a quandary as to whether to accept or not. I was making tremendous progress in my job at the Curriculum Branch. Our Native language pilot projects were underway, as was our work in social studies and other areas such as school broadcasts from the Department of Education. I wanted to see some programming that would be relevant to Native children in these broadcasts. There were so many areas to pursue and the political climate was right. On the other hand, I was vain enough to think I was the best person for such an important job with the MIB because I had been involved in Native education on a number of fronts, and I certainly did not want a non-Native taking on this work. After much deliberation, I made the decision to join the Manitoba Indian Brotherhood (now known as the Assembly of Manitoba Chiefs—a far more appropriate name). I know that the officials at the Department of Education were disappointed that I would be leaving after such a short period of time with them. So was I!

Fortunately, a couple of years earlier I had met Ida Wasacase, a Cree originally from Saskatchewan, who spent many years teaching in Whitehorse, Yukon, and had also spent several years as an exchange teacher in Soest, Germany. She had a reputation for being an excellent teacher. We became friends, and I thought of her as a possible replacement for me at the Curriculum Branch. I introduced her to the director of the Curriculum Branch, and she got the job. She was another person who taught many years on a teaching certificate and did not have a degree, though she did have a few university courses. This kind of situation would certainly not occur today. Hiring a person without going through a stringent interview process and hiring someone without a university degree for such a position is not an accepted practice. In fact, today, a minimum of a master's degree is the norm. It was, indeed, a different time. Ida did very well in the job, as she was a tireless, enthusiastic person who believed strongly that changes were necessary to improve Native education. Though she did not know her Cree language, she was a great support and motivator to those involved in the project. Ida stayed with the Curriculum Branch for three years and left her own mark.

It was an exciting time across the country as the chiefs decided to take matters into their own hands and challenge the federal government. What prompted this action was the Government of Canada's 1969 White Paper on Indians. It was during the time that Trudeau became prime minister and Jean Chrétien was the Minister of Indian Affairs. In Trudeau's attempt to bring about a "just society" he felt that everyone should have exactly the same rights and privileges. In essence, the intent was to remove the special status of Indians, and with it our special rights as derived from the treaties signed between the Queen of England and the Indians of Canada. The special rights were in lieu of giving up large tracts of land in Canada to be developed by people from other countries. The chiefs were aware that the White Paper was a breach of the treaties. There was a great uproar across the country, resulting in the Indians in each province and territory taking action by issuing position papers addressed to the government outlining how Indian people saw their ongoing relationship with the federal government in the areas of treaties and Aboriginal rights, land, hunting rights, the Indian Act, and culture. Further to this, our people stated what was expected in the areas of development that included health and social issues, housing, education, social development, legal protection, economic development, and reserve government.

We must have held at least four meetings of all the Manitoba chiefs in Winnipeg. Once I received the initial direction from the chiefs, I had to write up what they had proposed. We had a researcher on staff to assist us. Each director/writer went through this process. At subsequent meetings with the chiefs, I reviewed what I had written and we proceeded from there. This was a good process, as the chiefs were grouped according to language so that they could be better understood and be able to explain what they wanted without having to struggle with English. Many chiefs at that time were more proficient in their Native tongue than in English.

Our position paper, *Wahbung: Our Tomorrows*, was completed in October 1971. Other provincial and territorial Indian organizations had either completed or were in the process of preparing their responses to the federal government's White Paper. The first organization to complete its work was the Indians of Alberta, who referred to their paper as the "Red Paper," followed by British Columbia, calling their paper the "Brown Paper." Later, when I gave talks on *Wahbung*, I would say, "By the time we finished our paper, we had run out of appropriate colours."

It is worth noting excerpts of the positions and recommendations on education that we presented to the federal and provincial governments:

OUR POSITION (paraphrased):
We, the Indian people of Manitoba, believe in education:
—as a preparation for total living...;
—as a prime means of improving our economic and social conditions;
—as a means of providing the choice of where to live and work...;
—as a means of participating fully in our own social, economic, political and educational advancement;
—as a comprehensive program to meet the needs of the total community by including people of all ages.

OUR RECOMMENDATIONS (paraphrased)

—We call upon the federal government to make a clear declaration recognizing their financial obligation and responsibility for the education of Indian people;

—There must be a transfer of educational control to the Indian bands;

—There must be parental participation;

—Research must be conducted by or controlled by the Indian organization representing the people;

—There must be stress on excellence in education.

Wahbung: Our Tomorrows (Manitoba Indian Brotherhood, 1971).

One specific recommendation that involved the provincial government was the call for a review of agreements made by the federal government with the Manitoba government in regard to education affecting Indian people. The review to be conducted was to recommend revisions, termination, or continuance of such existing agreements. Several joint school agreements existed at the time between the federal government and specific school divisions that later were replaced by a Master Tuition Agreement.

With this movement a new relationship developed whereby decisions affecting Indians were to be made by tripartite discussions that would include the Manitoba government, the Department of Indian Affairs, and MIB. As a result, it was my job to work with government representatives on the Master Tuition Agreement in education. The Deputy Minister of Education represented the province, the federal government was represented by their regional director of education, and I represented the MIB as the director of education. We had very amicable meetings. I worked diligently and always came prepared with revisions, usually additions I felt should be made. The bottom line of this agreement was the tuition fee the federal government was to pay the province for each Indian child who attended a public school. At that time, integration was being encouraged. Many of the reserve schools were being closed, and the children were being transported to nearby towns. The theory behind this direction was that Indian children would have a better opportunity if they attended public schools.

The Department of Indian Affairs would pay a tuition fee to the province for each Indian student in attendance in a public school. The tripartite Master Tuition Agreement would address this matter. In addition to addressing the matter of the tuition fee, I was determined to have included two commitments I felt would contribute to the success of Indian children in public schools: (1) to hire paraprofessionals for schools where Indian children attended when requested by the band school authority, which at the time was usually a school committee; and (2) to provide funds for the preparation of appropriate and relevant materials and resources to schools attended by Indian children when requested by the band school authority. Both of these clauses were included in the Master Tuition Agreement. As a result, many more paraprofessionals, known as teachers' aides in the federal system, were hired over the years. As with Indian Affairs, many went on to become qualified teachers. Having money available, a greater effort was made by several schools to address the need for more relevant resources to address Indian education.

One serious result of the integration of children from the reserves, and Status Indians in general, was connected to the manner in which tuition payments were made to the province. The nominal enrolment in public schools was taken at the end of October and payment for the year was made on the basis of the number of Indian students enrolled at that time. What appeared to happen over the years was that public schools made a great effort to keep the children from dropping out prior to October 31, but after that date no great efforts were made to keep them in school. This was evident in the number of children enrolled in June of the same school year. In fact, the dropout rate was very high. A second problem was that the federal government paid a higher tuition fee for children in special classes—that is, children who for whatever reason required extra assistance in learning. This resulted in a large majority of Indian children being labelled slow learners. I have been amazed at how the federal government has continued to this day to pay the province an increasingly larger amount for tuition fees without any apparent accountability from the province. It is a well-known fact that Indian children in general have not done well in public schools. I have stated many times that the Department of Indian Affairs is writing a blank cheque to the province. In fact, today, we have many band-controlled schools in Manitoba, and a constant source of contention is the fact that the province receives at least a third more per child for tuition than that allotted for a child in a band school.

While at the MIB, I initiated a study that we entitled "Education is Failing the Indian." Using a Local Initiatives Grant, I hired Aboriginal students to conduct a study examining what was happening to our children in twelve public schools located around the province. They found that many students were age-grade decelerated. Some were as many as three years behind their peers. There was a high drop-out rate. Students were asked to give reasons why they dropped out. Some of the answers were the attitude of principals, teachers, and counsellors. Other responses were they wanted to work or they feared failing. A disproportionate number were in slow-learner classes, which may have been a contributing factor. Our recommendation to the Department of Indian Affairs was to investigate all placements of students in public schools and to rectify the situation for proper placement.

It was difficult for students to find any resources that had anything to do with Native people. I initiated a library with only Native resources. We hired a librarian to scout out such resources, and our library, housed at the MIB offices, became known as "The People's Library," which sounds a bit communistic, but we were trying to make a point that this library belonged to Native people. The library still exists today with the same name and many valuable resources. It is now part of the Manitoba Indian Cultural Education Centre on Sutherland Avenue in Winnipeg.

As a result of a concern by our people and a carry-over from my work at the Curriculum Branch, I launched a study in 1973 to review authorized social studies textbooks for grades four to six listed in the provincial curriculum. I seconded Pat McManus from Indian Affairs to supervise Indian students hired for the project and Maggie Balfour, a Cree woman from Norway House, to be an advisor to the team. Our method for the study was based on the criteria used by Garnet McDiarmid and David Pratt in a book called *Teaching Prejudice* (1971), an analysis of social studies textbooks authorized for use in Ontario. It was an amazing exercise and revealed bias beyond belief. We found, for example, bias by disembodiment in *Canada, A New Land* by Edith Deyell, which stated, "A few Natives went home with him [Columbus]. They were souvenirs of his trip, as were the bright coloured birds, the tobacco plants, and the potatoes." Another example was bias by disparagement in *Indians of Canada* (Coles Canadiana Collection), describing the bourgeois buying poor-quality pemmican from the Indians to be like "Tak[ing] scrapings from the dirtiest outside of a very stale piece of cold roast beef, add to it lumps of tallow, rancid fat...then garnish all with human hair...and short hairs from dogs and oxen, and you have pemmican." Our lengthy report was an indication that many textbooks were riddled with bias of all descriptions. We entitled our report, *The Shocking Truth about Indians in Textbooks*.

The study was not completed during my tenure with the MIB, but when it was completed, my successor, Sharon Thomas, asked that I present the report at a meeting she had organized with officials from the provincial and federal governments. It was a damning report that showed much bias in textbooks and materials authorized for grades four to six. I had highlighted parts of the report for my presentation to illustrate how serious an offence this was to Native people. The recommendation that we made to the provincial government was that this bias in textbooks be addressed and that a committee be struck that would include Native people to review future books and materials that were proposed for authorization by the Manitoba government. The Minister of Education was unable to attend this meeting; it was ironic that in his place he sent the Minister of Corrections. While there were many corrections to be made, this was not in the jurisdiction of someone who was responsible for the prison system. Sadly, the province did not act on our report, though we learned that they had spoken to the company that published *Manitoba: Its Peoples and Places*, one of the books in question. We felt it was a slight not only to devote three pages to the Indians of Manitoba, but that those pages portrayed Indians negatively. They were suggesting that Indians did not work, and that they were lazy and less intelligent than the rest of the population. The publisher argued that this was the "discovery approach." We argued that nine- and ten-year-olds were not likely to grasp the approach. The solution was a directive from the Department of Education to schools to cut the three pages out of the textbook. Obliteration was just another form of bias. *The Shocking Truth about Indians in Textbooks* was widely circulated and became a valuable resource.

A further development occurred after all the provincial and territorial position papers were completed. The National Indian Brotherhood (NIB), the organization representing the provincial and territorial Indian organizations, coordinated an effort to present a national position on Indian education. What was amazing was the similarity of the content of the position papers. The NIB, to my knowledge, had not issued any directives about what should be addressed in the papers. I don't recall having any conversation with any other organization regarding education. Communication was not like it is today. We did not have fax machines or the Internet, and most communication would be by telephone or Canada Post. Anyway, we were all too busy addressing our own issues to do anything else.

With these position papers in hand, the NIB had the ammunition it needed to deal with the federal government's stand on Indian education. The Trudeau government was halted in its tracks. In the history of relations between the Indians and the Crown, this was the first concerted national effort issued by the Indians to challenge the government's direction.

The NIB seconded Dr. Jacquie Weitz from the Department of Indian Affairs to spearhead the preparation of a national Indian education policy. Jacquie had spent time teaching in the Yukon and had great understanding and empathy for our situation. She formed a committee comprised of the education directors of the various organizations. This meant several trips to Ottawa where we met at the NIB offices. We found that all the provincial and territorial organizations expressed the need for Indian parents to be more involved in the education of their children. Up to this point, Indian Affairs could arbitrarily decide on the direction Indian education would take, as we experienced through residential schools and then the integration plan. We did not want any more of this paternalism. The committee put together a draft of our findings and our proposed action. It would go back to the NIB executive committee for their reaction. Even with this process, we tabled this landmark education policy paper, *Indian Control of Indian Education*, with Indian Affairs on December 21, 1972. On February 2, 1973, in a letter to NIB president George Manuel, the minister gave official recognition to *Indian Control of Indian Education*, approving its proposals and committing the Department of Indian Affairs (and Northern Development) to implementing them. That was a remarkable breakthrough!

A YEAR AT UNIVERSITY

In 1973, I decided it was time for me to go to the University of Manitoba full-time. From 1967 until then, I had only managed to complete part of my Bachelor of Arts by correspondence and summer school, due to the demands of my jobs. I was able to complete my Arts requirements by May of 1974, and I carried on until the end of August, completing as many education courses as I could. I continued to work on my courses through summer school and received my Bachelor of Education in 1976. It was my first and only experience going to university full-time. I was almost forty years old, had worked for many years, and knew how to concentrate on my work. Using my life experiences proved to be beneficial, as I completed many assignments and made class presentations about the Indian situation. I completed my master's degree in similar fashion—taking summer-school courses and graduating in 1980 at the age of forty-five.

For my Bachelor of Arts, I majored in sociology and minored in anthropology. A few courses stand out in my mind. I took a course in political science since I had been involved in a political organization, the Manitoba Indian Brotherhood. I was curious to learn what the academics had to say about politics. One day I met Marion Meadmore as I was on my way to one of my classes. She is a Cree about my age originally from Saskatchewan. We found that we were both enrolled in the same political science course, though not with the same professor. We had a friendly challenge about getting an A in the course. I enjoyed my class and worked hard to get an A to meet Marion's challenge. As it turned out, we both received As. Marion went on to become a lawyer.

I took a course in communication. This was an extremely dull course and the only class I did not bother to attend regularly. I did my assignments, one of which was an oral presentation to the class on Indian education. Well, I had it all over the young ones on this one, as I had been public speaking for at least ten years. My classmates seemed truly interested, and the professor gave me an A in the course, even with my poor attendance.

One summer I took a very interesting course in religion. I had to read a total of about thirty books in the course of six weeks. I was staying at my friend Pat McManus's home in Windsor Park during that summer. Her mother had been a kindergarten teacher and was interested in education. She offered to read some of the books so we could discuss them. They were books by Sarte, Ayn Rand, Dostoyovsky, and others. One of the assignments was to write a lengthy paper on a topic of our choice. Once again I turned to my experience and wrote a paper that I entitled, "My Country 'Tis of Thy People We're Dying" (the title taken from a popular song by Buffy Sainte-Marie). I wrote of the conditions of the Indian people of Canada and what we were doing to try to improve the situation. I quoted Harold Cardinal, a young Cree leader in Alberta, extensively. His book *The Unjust Society* (1969) was a response to Prime Minister Trudeau's "just society." I got an A-plus in that course, the only A-plus I would get in university.

Another paper I wrote I entitled, "If you are Seeking Utopia, the Only Way is the Indian Way." In this paper I shared some of the teachings of our people having to do with our values that included cooperation, listening, courage, humility, and respect for the wisdom of our elders, and so on.

I took an independent course with a professor named Erna Sawatsky at Brandon University. I had known Erna for some time, more by reputation than personally (she was known as an excellent teacher in northern Manitoba), and she knew my work. I approached her and suggested that I prepare a course outline for her on Indian education for use at the university. I did the work, and she gave me an A for my independent study. The course was accepted at Brandon University and remained on the books for a number of years.

I didn't have the usual university experience that one would have at a young age. I did not associate with anyone on the campus as I was years older than most of the students, and I did not bother to talk to my professors. I was renting an apartment on Taylor Avenue and would catch a bus on Waverley Street to go to my classes. I had a car, but it cost less to use the bus. I had saved enough money to see me through the year. I was not eligible for any assistance from Indian Affairs because I was a non-Status Indian. That did not matter to me; I was used to paying for my own education.

During this time, Bruce Sealey and I were completing our book *Indians Without Tipis*. We received a grant from the Canadian Studies Foundation. What prompted the writing of this book was that Bruce and I were tired of answering the same old questions over and over again. We were in positions where these questions were posed to us almost daily. What is an Indian? What is a Métis? What is the difference? Why is alcohol such a problem to Natives? What do you mean by Native culture? We set about to address these questions by inviting Native people we knew to write certain sections. Dr. Ahab Spence, a well-versed and respected Cree leader and Anglican priest wrote the chapter on "Indian Culture." Earl Duncan, a recovering alcoholic who had been sober for a number of years and was now a counsellor with the Alcoholism Foundation of Manitoba, wrote about "Alcohol and the Indian"; Joe Keeper, a community development officer originally from Norway House wrote about "Problems of Indian and Metis in Rural Areas." Bruce and I wrote a number of chapters. Bruce concentrated on writing about the history of Indian and Métis people in Canada while I wrote chapters related to Indian and Métis education. The cover of the book was done by the now famous Odawa artist Odjig, whose English name is Daphne Beavon. The book was published in 1973. It well may have been the first resource and reference book ever published by Native people in Canada. Later, Flora Zaharia, another educator of our generation, got a grant from the same source to prepare a kit for use by schools. It was known as *Tawow*. Our book became part of the kit.

THE NATIONAL INDIAN BROTHERHOOD

It was during that year of study that I received a phone call from Clive Linklater, who was the vice-president of the National Indian Brotherhood. Clive was a teacher by trade, and I had met him over the years at conferences. He was an Ojibway from Fort Frances, Ontario. He was among the few Indians across Canada who began teaching around the time I did in the 1950s. As such, he was a leader and had by the 1970s worked his way into the political arena. His call was to ask me to come to Ottawa to work as the education director for the NIB. It had never occurred to me to move away from Manitoba to work. Clive said that they wanted me to work with the education directors in the provincial and territorial organizations to promote the new policy of Indian Control of Indian Education. Having been involved in drafting the policy, I found this an exciting offer, and I accepted. As soon as I completed my coursework in August, I prepared to leave for Ottawa. This was a big move for me as I had been settled in Winnipeg for a few years.

The NIB had a small staff at that point. I was its first education director. Jacquie Weitz, who had been seconded from Indian Affairs to coordinate the work on developing the policy Indian Control of Indian Education, remained on the staff as a consultant. We worked very closely together throughout my years with the NIB. George Manuel was the president of the organization. Besides the education portfolio, there were directors of health, economic development, self-government, and social development. Each program area had a secretary. There were fewer than twenty of us on staff, including the secretaries and the receptionist.

This was an important time in the history of Indian-government relations because we had very clear directions provided by the position papers of the provincial and territorial Indian organizations, and none clearer than our education policy. George was the kind of leader who trusted his staff to do their jobs, and he was always prepared to back us up if we encountered problems in our dealings with Indian Affairs. My main contact was the director of education in Indian Affairs. George and Clive dealt with the top brass, such as the director general of Indian Affairs, who at one point in time was Bob Connelly. Bob had been a regional director of Indian Affairs for Manitoba. He was also a Manitoban who understood the Indian situation and was well respected by the Indians of our province. George and Clive also dealt directly with Prime Minister Trudeau and his cabinet.

All of us travelled a lot to the provinces and territories, keeping the grassroots informed and helping the communities in whatever way we could. Whenever George returned from one of his trips, he would call a meeting in the boardroom to tell us about his trip and the developments that were happening. He believed in sharing his experiences from the field and would discuss the challenges faced by our people as they moved toward self-sufficiency.

Money was at a premium, which meant we were a small staff with low pay. George was paid $25,000, and the rest of us were paid that amount or less.

Probably any one of us could have commanded more pay in any other job. The people in the NIB were dedicated to the cause and we all worked very hard. Our salaries certainly did not compare to what the civil servants, our counterparts in Indian Affairs, were getting paid.

Making the policy of Indian Control of Indian Education known to all reserves was no small feat. I worked closely with the education directors in the provinces and territories and often held workshops and conferences to discuss the policy and how it might be implemented. This landmark policy provided the opportunity for Indian Bands to take charge of the education on their reserves. I felt that adequate preparation time was needed for each community that decided they wanted to take over, and I negotiated with the Department of Indian Affairs to provide funding for this process. I felt that at least three years of preparation time would be needed before the bands would be ready. In my view, two things had to happen. One was to evaluate the current situation as it stood under Indian Affairs that had been running our schools for 100 years, and it was obvious that they were not doing a good job. Very few students were completing high school. In fact the dropout rate was over 90 percent. Even prior to the government White Paper of 1969, our people's dissatisfaction with education was evident. This prompted a review of Indian education by a standing committee of the House of Commons.[1] The statistics were startling, even by their own admission. It found a dropout rate four times the national average (96 percent of Indian children never finished high school), "inaccuracies and omissions" relating to the Indian contribution to Canadian history in texts used in federal and provincial schools, an age-grade retardation, which accelerated as the child progressed through primary and elementary grades, less than 15 percent of the teachers had specialized training in cross-cultural education and less than 10 percent had any knowledge of Indian languages, and the majority of Indian parents were uninformed about the implication of transferring children from reserve schools to provincial schools.

The policy, then, was timely. It put education into the hands of the parents, and "parental responsibility and local control" became our mantra. No

1. Report of the Standing Committee on Indian Affairs, House of Commons, June 22, 1971.

more would we accept arbitrary directions taken by Indian Affairs. The process that had to precede takeover was based on documenting the state of education under the government prior to takeover; otherwise, how would we know what progress we were making? We had to identify our starting point because we were inheriting problems created by Indian Affairs.

In communities that requested my services, I held community workshops that were usually three days long to address the second very important point that the bands had to consider: how were they going to do things differently to effect positive change? I had worked with Clive Linklater on conducting workshops in other situations. As a trained facilitator, he taught me a lot about how to arrive at certain goals by using a structured-experience approach. It was a great way to handle these workshops on Indian control. Basically, we dealt with four questions that were designed by Clive: Where are we now? Where do we want to go? How will we get there? How will we know when we are there? For example, in asking "where are we now?" I divided the participants into groups of five or six and had them work together, using flip chart paper and felt pens of various colours. I instructed them to draw a path or river to illustrate the history of education in their community as they remembered it. This provided an opportunity for all persons in the group to share their views. This would be followed by reports from each of the groups. Then, in a plenary session we would talk about the similarities in the reports that provided the base we needed to answer the question. I often used a fantasy exercise to work with our second question, "Where do we want to go?" I divided them into groups different from the first exercise and ask them to consider what they thought would be an ideal education for their community. I asked them to avoid using written sentences, but rather to use symbols or single words to illustrate their points on a large sheet of paper. Many very interesting ideas were presented, with one or two people reporting back to the larger group. And so the process continued over the course of three days. I preferred to have only twenty-five to thirty participants at each workshop so that it was manageable and, more importantly, that everyone present had an opportunity to speak.

These workshops were very effective. The community people participated willingly. The Elders took the process seriously and would often be there bright and early in the morning ready for the workshop. It gave an opportunity for all ages of parents and grandparents to take part. It was clear that they were aware of the problem and that they had ideas about what would constitute a quality education for their children. Culture was the dominant factor throughout, since that was the main element missing under the system provided by the Department of Indian Affairs.

The Department of Indian Affairs ceased to provide funding for this preparation phase. They had their own agenda about preparation. Their approach was to turn over, in piecemeal fashion, certain duties to bands. They began by putting bands in charge of the janitorial services. This was not what we had in mind. It was clear from the outset that, although the Department of Indian Affairs had approved the policy and committed itself to fulfilling the demands outlined in the policy, they had a totally different interpretation of Indian control. They did not plan to do it our way. The federal government's plan was to gradually turn over responsibility to the bands, resulting in nothing more than having Indians run Indian Affairs programs. This was a constant battle that continues to this day.

During those years, I made many speeches at education conferences across the country on Indian Control of Indian Education. This policy impacted education dramatically because finally parents' voices were to be heard and acted upon. The policy contained a statement of our people's philosophy, goals, principles, and directions. The two main principles were "parental responsibility" and "local control." It recognized that Indian parents must enjoy the same fundamental decision-making rights about their children's education as other parents across Canada. It called for radical change to make education relevant to the philosophy and needs of the Indian people. Indian people want education to give their children a strong sense of identity, with confidence in their personal worth and ability.

The policy stated:

We believe in education:
...as a preparation for total living
...as a means of free choice of where to live and work
...as a means of enabling us to participate fully in our

own social, economic and educational advancement.
(National Indian Brotherhood, 1972)

It was a four-point policy dealing with responsibility, programs, teachers, and facilities and services. It called for the training of Indian teachers; changes in the curriculum to reflect the culture and values of our people; nursery schools and kindergartens; vocational, adult, and post-secondary education; the use of Indian languages as languages of instruction; and need for cultural education centres. This watershed document drastically changed the landscape of Indian education, and more teacher training programs emerged at various universities, as did Native Studies departments. Ministers of Education across the country examined their curricula and worked to accommodate changes. Most of all, more schools that included high-school grades were built on reserves. As a result, the high-school completion rate improved. Despite the obstacles faced by dealing with the Indian Affairs department over the years, progress has been made. The strong influence of our position paper, *Wahbung*, can be seen throughout Indian Control of Indian Education.

Jim and I continued to keep company while I worked at the NIB. Before I arrived in Ottawa, Jim had moved there to work at Indian Affairs headquarters. Our jobs gave us some problems in our relationship, as he was employed by the Department of Indian Affairs and had responsibilities related to the policy. We had several opposing views on how the policy of Indian control would be enforced. As I mentioned earlier, Indian Affairs' idea was to transfer education over to the Indian Bands, while the Indian view was to create a new system. One of our disagreements involved the education circulars, intended to guide the process. In all, the department created twelve circulars that became known as Education Circulars E1 to E12. The circulars covered everything from how the school floors should be cleaned using Dust Bane Sweeping Compound to post-secondary education funding. The NIB rejected the circulars E1 to E11 outright as they were an infringement on our policy to control our own education. It was a battle that we finally won. We decided we had to deal with the E12 circular on post-secondary education because the government determined that this was not a right covered by treaty. The treaties (written in the late 1800s to early 1900s) stated that the government would build schools when they were requested. The government took that to mean up to grade twelve and anything beyond that was discretionary or "out of the goodness of their hearts." The education directors worked with their bands and the national office to revise the E12 circular. Indian university students, mainly from Trent University, got involved, and they made recommendations to the executive committee of the NIB. Their voices were a strong support for funding for post-secondary education. We finally arrived at a reasonable compromise with Indian Affairs, and funding was secured with agreed-upon guidelines. The E12 circular was in existence for many years.

I stayed with the NIB for two years, from 1974 to 1976. We had accomplished a lot during those two years, and I left, along with several other staff members, when George Manuel decided not to run for re-election. He had been in the position for several years and he was exhausted. In retrospect, I realize that it was an ill-conceived plan for so many of us to be leaving the NIB at the same time. George had worked with Prime Minister Trudeau effectively, and they had created a Joint NIB-Cabinet committee to deal with resolving the challenges being faced by the Indians of Canada. The main issue on the table was Indian education. Here we were at the table with the very senior Cabinet ministers of the government. As the education director, and a member the joint NIB/DIA sub-committee to study this problem and make recommendations, I was in attendance at these meetings to follow the proceedings. I was very impressed with our elected leadership, the presidents of our provincial and territorial organizations who formed the NIB executive, who could debate with the best of them. Harold Cardinal, a young educated leader of the Indian Association of Alberta, was a shining light and could effectively challenge the government side.

The issue was the Indian Act, which we believed was a deterrent to implementing the policy of Indian Control. The Act states that the federal government could enter into agreements with the provincial government, commissioners of the territorial governments, public or private schools, religious organizations, and charitable organizations. Indian bands were not included. That means that the Minister of Indian Affairs is ultimately responsible for education, even if controlled by the Indian bands. We wanted our bands to be more autonomous, to set new directions without government interference, and to be able to deal directly with Treasury Board and other government departments without going through the Minister of Indian Affairs. The joint NIB/DIA sub-committee was involved in many meetings, and each side had a lawyer. Members of the committee were drawn from the NIB executive, one of whom was Sol Sanderson of the Federation of Saskatchewan Indians, a strong advocate in Indian education. Specifically, our task was to revise Sections 114 to 123 of the existing Indian Act that dealt with education. What was amazing was that the government had agreed that it would be possible to revise a part of the Indian Act. The process was going well, and we felt we were getting satisfactory results. Periodically, the committee presented interim reports to the joint NIB-Cabinet committee co-chaired by the prime minister and the president of the NIB. While proposed directions were strongly debated, the process was never stalled. We were making progress, though it took time, as these things tend to do, especially when working with government.

To this day, I have no idea how we all could abandon ship at the same time. It was a disastrous move. The end result was that a new president was elected for the NIB. In time, the joint NIB-Cabinet committee was disbanded and the work of our joint working committee to revise the Indian Act was lost. I often wonder how different the policy of Indian Control of Indian Education would look today had that revision to the Indian Act been accomplished. It is clear that the clause we intended to include, which would authorize the Minister of Indian Affairs to enter into agreements with Indian bands for the education of their children, would have enabled bands more creativity in setting up a quality education system.

TRAVELLING TO ISRAEL

I am fortunate to have travelled to many parts of the world. Each place had its own story and its own beauty, as I saw on my pilgrimage to the Holy Land in 1978. It was organized by a United Church minister who was a former principal of the Rossville Residential School in Norway House before my time there. He and his wife and daughter had made this pilgrimage previously.

My friend Pat and her mother came along as well. I know this is something my mother would have enjoyed, as she was a strong Christian, and I did invite her. She said that my dad had not been feeling well and she did not want to leave him. I know that she was also very afraid of flying, though I did get her on a plane once to Norway House.

I was deeply moved while in the Holy Land, seeing places I had heard of so many times at Sunday school and church. Here I was seeing where Jesus was born in the city of Bethlehem, where he grew up in Jerusalem, where he was crucified, and the tomb where he was buried. Some experiences stand out in my mind, like the time we were in the Garden of Gethsemane having a service, when suddenly it became dark, though it was mid afternoon. I thought this was not unlike what I understood happened when Jesus was crucified. It was like a huge cloud had rolled over the place. The spot believed to be where Jesus was born was marked by a circular marble area with lamps hanging down over a star that marked the centre. I found it far too ornate and not anything like the humble stable we read about. We stopped at the Dead Sea, and it was a great surprise to find out just how dense the Dead Sea is. We were able to get in the water which was so buoyant that it was impossible to sink, This was great for me, as I was not a swimmer at that time.

In Jordan, we went to the Jordan River, where several members of our group were baptized. I brought back a small bottle of holy water for my parents. Here we also went to visit the fascinating "lost city" of Petra, believed to have been the centre of the silk trade in much earlier times. Petra was in its early stages of restoration, and the excavation of various buildings was just becoming visible. To get to the site we had to go by horseback because the Siq, an early waterway, had left behind little, rounded rocks that were difficult to walk on, at least for tourists. Our horses were led by local men. Petra was pink stone like I had never seen before.

Then at another point when we were on a boat trip on the Sea of Galilee on a day when the weather seemed calm, we were suddenly hit by a storm carrying with it a strong wind that rocked the boat. I had on a light coat that was blowing in the wind. I have a photo of me clinging to my coat. This reminded me of how we learned that Jesus stilled the waters on that sea. On returning to Jerusalem, I also visited the Western Wall, referred to as the Wailing Wall, and put a message in the wall as is the custom.

Of course, we saw the pyramids and the sphinx in Egypt and went on a camel ride. It was a surprise to be entertained in Cairo by belly dancers who were middle-aged women who could not be described as slender.

I have only skimmed over all that we saw and experienced. It is sufficient to say that I am glad that I had the privilege of being there. Among other souvenirs, I brought back Bibles for my father and mother. The one for my dad had a cover made of olive wood and my mother's was mother of pearl. Both are in my possession now.

FREELANCE CONSULTANT

After leaving the National Indian Brotherhood, I remained in Ottawa working as a freelance Indian education consultant. Much of my work included working with bands across the country that planned to take control of education in their communities. I was involved in school evaluations, part of the initiative to find out the state of education in schools before bands took over. I was in demand. I did workshops with Indian Affairs staff at high levels as well. The intention was to sensitize staff to Indian culture and issues. Clive and I often presented these workshops together.

While at the NIB, Clive and I had conducted a one-week workshop for all of the NIB staff, from the elected officials to the secretaries. It was designed to set short- and long-term goals for the organization. We met at Smiths Falls, in a residential setting where we would not be distracted by our work in Ottawa. Our sessions were from 9 a.m. to 12 noon, 2 p.m. to 5 p.m., and again from 7 p.m. to 10 p.m., a total of nine hours a day. Everyone was required to be present, prompt, and to participate. We engaged in the kind of structured experiences that encouraged participation from everyone present. It was George's philosophy that we were all equal, no matter what our particular jobs were. We accomplished a lot during that time and came away with our short- and long-term goals in place.

I used this process learned from Clive Linklater to do a three-day workshop for the Native Women's Association of Canada. What was basic to all these workshops was that the goals and objectives of the organizations were clear. At the conclusion, the group should have identified how to achieve their goals and objectives and an implementation process. I enjoyed doing these workshops and used this process for many years.

At this point I had enrolled in a Master of Education program at the University of Manitoba at the urging of Bruce Sealey. It was my intention to take summer school courses. I had completed two courses and got As in both of them. In 1977, I decided to enroll in an evening course at the University of Ottawa. I wanted to get on with my studies while still being able to work. I also was curious to see if I could score an A in courses at another university. It was a grind to take courses while freelancing, as my work often required me to be away from Ottawa but I got As in both courses.

During this time, in 1978, I met Cecil Smith, a member of Parliament for the Churchill riding in Manitoba. He asked me if I knew anyone who might be interested in working for him as a research assistant in his Ottawa office. My cousin Pat Beyer and I were sharing an apartment at the time. I told her about Cecil's request and asked her if she knew anyone who might be interested. Then I said, "Maybe I should take it." Fisher River, my home reserve, was in the Churchill riding, and I thought it would be an interesting experience. I know Cecil did not expect me to want the job since these positions were often offered to very junior people, usually just starting out. I called him up and said to him, "Hi Cecil. About that job you spoke of, how about me?" "You?" he responded, and I confirmed my offer. He said it didn't pay much, but we decided to meet to talk about it. He wanted someone to respond to some of his mail, to take some of his phone calls, and attend meetings. He had a regular secretary, but he wanted someone who could answer routine enquiries. Since the salary was just over $8,000, I knew I couldn't live on that alone. I suggested that he allow me to do some contract work at the same time and spend just two or three days in his office. While the money was nothing, the experience I received during that time was immeasurable. When I left the job, a year later, I received a bonus cheque, as I should have had a slightly higher wage because I did have two degrees by then.

I checked Cecil's in-box and answered whatever correspondence I could. He briefed me on some of the enquiries. The communiques that came in the mail taught me much about what was going on in the government. Even backbenchers such as Cecil were privy to all kinds of information. During that time, the Otineka Mall was being built in Opaskwayak, Manitoba. I went on the radio in northern Manitoba, talking about the mall in Cree, telling the people of Cecil's positive response to the new development.

It was also after the James Bay Cree had signed the James Bay and Northern Quebec Agreement. The Naskapi Indians did not feel that they were fairly considered in the deal and were given an opportunity to be heard by the Indian Affairs Standing Committee, a committee made up of elected officials. Cecil asked me to attend these meetings as an observer. Some of the representatives of the Naskapi spoke through an interpreter. Since it is an Algonquin language, as is Cree, I was able to understand a bit of the language. It was an interesting process and, in the end, the Naskapi were successful in having some of their demands met.

I prepared monthly bulletins to be sent to the constituents, and attended the meetings of the Standing Committee on Indian Affairs, where various issues were covered. I also went to many sessions of Question Period, as Cecil wanted to be up-to-date, and quite often he would be away in the riding on those days. Churchill was one of the largest ridings in the country, if not the largest, in terms of area.

Every so often, the Opposition has an opportunity to present issues to the Parliament. It was decided in June of 1978 to have an Opposition Day devoted to questions regarding Indian education. I was asked to write up a number of questions that would address the serious situation Indian education was in. As it turned out, all of the questions used by members of the Opposition were mine. I kept a copy of this particular *Hansard* for many years.

Prior to this experience, I had very little knowledge of the parliamentary process and not a whole lot about politics in general. I knew about our dealings with the government civil service, in particular our dealings with the Department of Indian Affairs. I also had the privilege of being at the joint NIB-Cabinet meetings led by George Manuel. Apart from that, I knew little. The experience of working on Parliament Hill and working from an office in the Confederation Building shed much light on the workings of government. My interest in politics, elections, and policies has continued to this day. I even watch United States politics, and was especially interested when Barack Obama came on the stage.

Working on Parliament Hill had its perks. There was a dining room in the Confederation Building that offered subsidized meals. I quite often ate my evening meal there since I frequently worked late. There is a little green bus that goes back and forth from the various buildings on the Hill. There was no need to go outside and walk from the Confederation Building to the Centre Block, where I often had to go, in the cold and rain. I began to feel that I could be an MP, and gave it consideration. I was encouraged by George Manuel to run for parliament. Cecil was stepping down, and I thought of running in Churchill. However, there was a snap election, and I had no time to prepare and had other commitments at the time. I have often wondered how such a move might have affected the course of my life. Basically, I think of myself as an educator first, and do not regret my decision to keep on that path.

One summer I had planned to go to the University of Manitoba to take my last required course. As it turned out, I was too heavily committed to be able to attend. I was able to have the course deferred and I did an independent study with Dr. Rodney Clifton, then a professor at Memorial University in St. John's, Newfoundland. It was his course that I had missed at the University of Manitoba, where he was a visiting professor. I took two weeks away from my work, flew to St. John's, and had one-on-one meetings with Dr. Clifton. He loaded me down with readings that we discussed. I enjoyed the course and completed with an A. Now the next hurdle would be to do my thesis. In 1978, I was finished my course work and ready to begin my master's thesis.

During this consultancy period I had an opportunity to work on a contract with the Evaluation Branch of Department of Indian Affairs. I was asked to evaluate Indian education in Manitoba. I was to compare what was happening in federal Indian Affairs schools, public schools, and band schools. There were few band schools in existence at that time, but they were included. I visited a number of public schools. It was suspected that the Indian children in public schools were not doing well. I found that many were being placed in special education classes in the elementary grades and in occupational entrance programs in high school. Placement in these classes meant that Indians were seen to have learning difficulties and could not handle regular course work. As I mentioned earlier, a higher tuition fee was paid to the provincial government for Indian children in slow-learner classes. The legitimacy of these placements was questionable.

I made it a point to meet with the parents who sent their children to the schools that formed part of my study. In one instance, the parents of a particular reserve took immediate action when they heard the alarming news of so many of their children being placed in slow-learner classes. They met with the school board to seek answers and solutions to the situation. They knew that this was a disproportionate number to be classified as slow learners. Typically, 3 percent of a given population might fall into this category. When they could not reach a satisfactory solution, they pulled their children out of that school and moved them to another school nearby. Before transferring their children, they made clear to the school administration their expectations regarding a proper education for their children. Language could not be blamed for keeping the children in slow-learner classes as they all had English as their first language, having lived in southern Manitoba. I was pleased that these parents took strong action. Indian Affairs had to respect their choices, given the circumstances. This is what was intended with the policy of Indian Control of Indian Education. Parental responsibility and local control meant that parents would play an active role in the education of their children. This was difficult to do in the public school situation. We had stated in *Indian Control of Indian Education* that where children attended public schools, a member of the children's reserve should be on the school board. Few school boards responded to this direction.

In my evaluation of particular high schools, I found a similar situation where most Indian students were placed in the occupational entrance stream. What was most alarming at one public high school was that the Department of Indian Affairs had entered into an agreement to fund the building of a gymnasium because of the number of Indian students in that school. In reviewing the statistics, I found that over a period of nearly twenty years the school had only graduated three Indian students from high school. At another public school I asked about how they were addressing the needs of Indian children, and did they have any cultural materials? They had the nerve to point out an archery set that was regarded as cultural.

I visited a number of Indian Affairs schools and found that they fared slightly better than the public schools in terms of addressing the needs of Indian children. I visited the few band schools in operation. My conclusion, no doubt biased, was that band schools were better suited to directing the education of their children.

My completed report was entitled, *Education of Indian Children in Federal, Provincial and Band Schools in Manitoba* (1978). The director of the Evaluation Branch called it "a bestseller" and stated that it impacted the way education services were provided to Indian children. No doubt, it helped educators, researchers, and Indian communities.

I continued to work on my thesis, but with my busy schedule my work was stalled for periods of time and I felt like giving up on it. Once again, Bruce Sealey was my mentor, urging me to complete the work. I finally got it done and had my oral presentation in November 1980 before a panel of three professors with a number of observers present. All went well, and I had successfully completed my master's degree. I was now forty-five years old.

In the spring of 1978, I went riding motorcycle with Jim, who had adopted two Cree boys from Saskatchewan, with the intention of finding a place where we could take the boys for weekends to get them out of the city. The boys were nine and eleven and had been in foster care when Jim adopted them. In our search, we came upon a place called Holiday Ranch. It was a campground, and not at all what we were looking for, but somehow it caught our fancy. Not that it looked at all attractive; it was springtime and the buildings were in need of repair. It had a main building that housed the store, the office, and a restaurant. The basement of the building was for recreation, though it was only crudely finished. There was a large, unattractive building used for storage just in front of the main building. It also had five cottages and a marina. But it was well situated on White Lake, with cottagers all around the lake. The possibilities it offered got us thinking. At the time, Jim was still with Indian Affairs and I was a freelance consultant; we had some extra money. Jim had bought a new house. After Jim bought the new house and before he adopted the boys, we had talked about marriage. By then we had been keeping company for at least ten years. We were a strange pair, both totally dedicated to our jobs that obviously came first. We had talked about adopting after we were married. It should have been an ideal situation, but it didn't work out that way. I decided it was best to keep on the way we were. I could not make the commitment, and I must have instinctively known that I would follow my passion for education wherever it led me.

Together with Jim's brother, Peter, and sister-in-law, we bought the thirteen-acre property. We saw it as a place where members of our families could work, and would certainly be a great place for Jim's boys. We were in possession of the campground by that summer. Danny, Peter's son, who was a university student, became the manager. His daughter Susan, also a university student, came to work. My brother Reggie came from Manitoba to take charge of the marina. He had some familiarity with boats, as our father was a fisherman. My sister Darlene also came to work as a cleaning lady. A number of people who had been camping there over the years continued to come, some from as far away as Wisconsin. There was a lot to do to improve the place, which we named Cedar Cove Park and referred to as "the park." Jim commuted daily from Cedar Cove to Ottawa, a one-hour drive each way. We left things to Danny and company during the week, but Jim and the boys were living there, so he was able to oversee the park. They lived in a suite in the lodge for a number of years. On the weekends, all four of us owners were often at Cedar Cove; weekends were the busiest times. I am not at all good in the kitchen, but that first summer I found myself in the kitchen making pizzas. We were taking orders from the campers, and I was kept busy. It was a fun time and a challenging venture.

Jim took early retirement after five years of commuting daily to Ottawa, although you could still find him going to Ottawa to buy supplies on the weekends. He became a full-time manager of the park. After his father passed away in 1980 in Saskatoon, his mother moved to Cedar Cove. A cottage was built for her, and while she was able she helped out by going to pick up the worms needed for bait and pick up the booze in Arnprior, a town a half hour away. I continued to visit Cedar Cove over the years (and I even lived there for two years after my retirement), but it was really Jim's life and love. He would run the campground that had grown to 100 acres and classified as a "triple-A" resort until it sold in 2006.

"NOT A PROPHET IN YOUR OWN LAND"

During my Christmas vacation at Fisher River in 1977, I received a call at my parents' home from one of the band councillors, asking if I could meet with the council before I returned to Ottawa. We agreed to meet on December 26—I knew that they had to have something important to discuss with me to do it on Boxing Day. They were all present for the meeting. They knew the major role I had played in the development and implementation of Indian Control of Indian Education. They wanted to know, would I help them take over their education?

I really did not want to leave Ottawa, but in the end I felt I could not refuse my own community. After all, I was known as "Miss Indian Control of Indian Education." I had commitments for the coming year and could not just pack up and leave. I told the band council that I would consider their proposal, but that I would not be available until the following September. The council was in touch with me again in late spring. I learned that an election for chief and councillors was to be held in August. The way band elections work at Fisher River is that all are declared vacancies and any incumbents can run for re-election. I knew enough about band politics to suggest we wait until after the election to see if the new slate of officers would want to go ahead with the education takeover.

The chief was re-elected, and all but one councillor—the one who had initially contacted me—were not re-elected. I joined the council for a meeting in Winnipeg to discuss the project. It was agreed that I would begin in September 1978. I bought a thirteen-foot ATCO trailer in Winnipeg and had it set up in my parents' yard. With a few repairs and the bottom insulated and skirted, it would be sufficient to withstand the cold winter. The band council provided the labour to make the trailer habitable.

I was assigned an office in the band office. There were only a handful of employees, as was typical of the day. A general office provided secretarial and financial duties for the council members and other program directors. Having worked with a number of Indian bands in the planning for takeover, I now had the opportunity to engage those ideas first-hand with my own people.

One of the first things I had to do was to familiarize the community members with the policy of Indian Control of Indian Education and what taking over education could mean to them and their children. I had emphasized with the chief and council that they had to be actively involved in the process. I would brief them on our progress at their weekly meetings, and they would give me feedback on our plans. The chief and council were critical to this process because, as the policy reads, the government would pass on legal responsibility for the administration of funds to a band council, the legal entity of the reserve.

The job ahead was immense, more than I could handle alone. I thought about who might be interested in assisting me with the job. I remembered having met Chuck Hudson, a member of the Fisher River band who was working as an administrator at the Saskatchewan Indian Federated College. His field of study was education, and he had alluded to the fact he would like to work at Fisher River someday. I was given approval to hire Chuck as my assistant. Between the two of us, I felt I could put the plan together and carry it out. I had an ulterior motive in hiring Chuck: I had told the band council that I was planning to stay at Fisher River for no longer than three years. I knew Chuck would be the ideal person to continue the work and that his move to the reserve would be more permanent.

We launched into a number of initiatives immediately. We organized a three-day workshop for parents and other community members. I asked the chief and councillors to attend; they were present for some of the time. The workshop was well attended and I was pleased that my mother came. I think she often wondered what I did after I left teaching. I recall her asking me one time, "Why don't you teach anymore?" It was hard for her to understand what I did as a supervisor of schools or a curriculum consultant; she saw teaching as the ultimate career.

Many years later, I found my mother's copy of the report of the workshop stored among her important papers. It was interesting to see the results. Among the participants were the band council and staff, school staff, grade twelve students, parents, grandparents, guardians, and other interested people. We had an activity to discuss ideas about what curriculum adaptations could be made to better meet the needs of the Fisher River students. Though they probably never entertained this question before, the participants made many suggestions, including using books and materials more relevant to the children's lives, having Cree integrated into other subjects, getting back to basics, and more. They also felt there should be a community library that would be open every day. When asked about science, it was suggested that a greenhouse be built; another response was to build a nuclear station (This was said jokingly). I remember how freely and intensely they participated. It got a bit political as well, with recommendations for an open band meeting and remarks that the chief and council should have been present for the duration of the workshop because all this was important. I later wondered whether this empowerment the local people were exhibiting had anything to do with what subsequently occurred.

As with other workshops held in communities, it was evident that the people knew that there was something wrong with the Indian Affairs system and had clear ideas of what was needed to provide a richer and more meaningful education for their children.

As there were no local teachers on the teaching staff at Fisher River, I began negotiations with Brandon University for a teacher-training program on our reserve. The Brandon University Northern Teacher Education Program (BUNTEP) was already established on a number of reserves at this point. Our chances looked very good. We started with a Native literature university course taught as a night course. I had a meeting with the school-bus drivers who had complained about being insufficiently paid. I raised the possibility of them getting their own buses and earning more revenue.

We had to prepare for a school board or some form of education authority, so we began training for potential board members. We discussed what a school board does, I had them visit classrooms to see what the children were doing, and, of course, how effective the teacher was. We really were well on our way. I kept the band council informed and I ensured that I was given time to speak at band council meetings. Things seemed to be going well, and the chief said, "I think you will have to stay longer than three years," which indicated to me that he was pleased with our progress. It seemed to me that we could be a model of how to go about the process for other communities. We were moving quickly, and all was going well, though we had only been in the process of takeover for three months.

Typically, band councils designate portfolios for each councillor including the chief. The councillor with the education portfolio, who was also the United Church minister, worked closely with us. In his council role, he suggested that it was time that we took over the education funds, an amount, I believe, that was around $60,000 (in 1979), which was not extensive. I wrote up a band council resolution (BCR) requesting the transfer of the funds so we could begin the process of taking care of education monies.

To this day, I'm not sure what triggered what was to follow. On December 19, 1979, I went to Winnipeg to defend my master's thesis. When I returned home that evening, I met one of the councillors, who said, "I want you to know I did not agree with what the council did today." In the mail, I found a registered letter written to me to say that my services were no longer required, that I had overstepped my mandate, and that the termination was effective immediately. It was signed by the chief and all but one councillor, the one with the education portfolio. As I was to learn later, he had been excluded from any meetings regarding this action. Chuck Hudson had received a similar letter to mine. We were both fired.

Devastated as we were about this sudden turn of events, Chuck and I continued to go to work every day, planning to do so until the Christmas vacation. The councillor who was left out of the process and I immediately asked for a meeting with the chief and council, but we were informed that the chief would be away until after Christmas. I knew that he was avoiding having to face us. The councillor continued to try to get a meeting; the council owed him an explanation too. Finally, I decided to press charges of wrongful dismissal. I was very torn over taking this action since I had come to Fisher River to help my people take an important step toward independence. I saw no other choice and I felt it necessary to go ahead. I hired a lawyer.

The next step was to give the chief a summons, which had to be delivered in person. After Christmas, I went to the band office and asked to see the chief. I was told he was busy, in a meeting, so I knew he was there. I marched straight into the boardroom and handed him the summons without a word. Not one thing was said; there was just stunned silence.

At the meetings for discovery, the chief and councillors' stories contradicted one another; they didn't have the facts straight. We had about three meetings on this issue, and it became apparent that they were not going to win this case. I was pleased, since I was already working in Vancouver and was not interested in continuing to have to return to Winnipeg. Finally, they agreed to pay any costs I incurred, along with a token amount of about $1,000. I could not claim loss of wages as I was hired immediately after I was fired.

I was well-known across Canada as an educator and I had a good reputation for getting things done. It amazed many people that I could be fired. One of the first calls I received was from the assistant deputy minister of Indian Affairs, suggesting I come to work for them at the department's headquarters in Ottawa. Another call came from the vice-president of Brandon University, also eager to hire me. I took the job offered to me by the Fairford Indian band, to do their school evaluation. I had to remain in Manitoba because my mother had just been diagnosed with melanoma.

After the fiasco with the chief and the council at Fisher River, I continued to be very busy with contract work. My dad had passed away with a heart attack on November 11, 1979, and now my mother had been diagnosed with cancer. After my dad died, my mother spent time in Winnipeg because she was under doctor's care and receiving radiation treatments. My sister Darlene was living in Winnipeg at the time with her two little girls. Darlene and I decided that she had to have a bigger space if Mom was to live with her while she was an outpatient. We rented a house on Smithfield Avenue, where she could have her own bedroom. I helped them with the rent. I had moved my trailer from Fisher River to a trailer park in North Kildonan, a Winnipeg suburb. While the Fisher River experience is the only extreme problem I encountered during my career, I have thought about it as divine guidance, to be with my parents before their deaths, though it did not lessen the pain of the experience.

CHAPTER FIVE

The University of British Columbia

NATIVE INDIAN TEACHER EDUCATION PROGRAM

During the spring of 1980, I received a phone call from Joe Handley, a Métis gentleman originally from Saskatchewan, working at the University of British Columbia. I had met Joe at one of the many education conferences we attended. He, too, had started out as a teacher. He was calling to tell me that the Native Indian Teacher Education Program (NITEP), in operation since 1971, was looking for a Native supervisor. The concept of teacher education programs for Native people had begun in the Northwest Territories in 1970, the first of many that would follow. The policy of Indian Control of Indian Education calling for more Native teachers had prompted universities to take action all across Canada.

NITEP may have been the second program to be initiated. Since its inception, it had been run by Dr. Art More, a non-Native who, with a number of Native students at the university, had lobbied for a teacher education program especially for Natives. NITEP was guided by an advisory committee made up of Native community leaders both rural and urban; the university assistant dean of education, Murray Elliot, and a member of the British Columbia Teachers' Federation; and the NITEP supervisor as an ex-officio member.

I was not immediately interested in the job. My consulting work was going well. I worked all across Canada, mainly doing evaluations of Indian Affairs schools where bands were planning to take over education. I did many workshops on Indian Control of Indian Education. I also did some work for government bodies on cultural sensitization. I decided to apply for the job at UBC, and was invited for an interview. This was a most interesting process. I arrived in Vancouver the night before and was put up at a downtown hotel. The next morning, Art More picked me up and briefed me on the day's schedule. I was to return to Winnipeg that evening, as I had commitments. The first on the list was a brief meeting with the dean, Dr. Roy Bently, and his associate dean, Doug McKie. An informal, cordial meeting followed in the staff lounge with a group of professors in education. They asked me a few questions.

I went for an early lunch to a cafeteria with the NITEP secretary and the financial clerk, which I thought a bit peculiar though pleasant. These fine young women had been with NITEP for a few years. From there, I was to give a noon-hour presentation that was open to whoever wished to hear me, or rather size me up. It was well attended. Then, the most important meeting was the formal interview with the members of the advisory committee. I gathered that they had done a search in BC, as their preference was a BC Native but they were unable to identify anyone. One of the questions was, "Would you try to get more BC Native people on the NITEP staff?" At the time there were only three Native people on staff—a secretary, a financial clerk, and a counsellor. The counsellor was Caroline Bugge, the first NITEP graduate. I told them that I was certainly willing to do that and that I would accept a three-year contract if chosen. I had met Robert (Bob) Sterling, the chairman of the committee, at previous Native education conferences; he was well aware of my work and reputation. Robert had been one of the people instrumental in the creation of NITEP and had been the chair since its inception. Though he knew me, he kept silent throughout the interview, letting the other members question me. Joan Ryan, also part of the founding group, had been a coordinator for NITEP sometime during these years. She seemed particularly aggressive in questioning me. I felt that she resented the fact that a prairie Cree was applying for the job. Joan was a teacher in a public school, one of the first wave of teachers around my time in the 1950s.

Joan became my staunchest supporter and a great help in my job. She never ceased being critical, but as I later found when I got to know her better, it was her way of providing constructive support. She was protecting the turf of NITEP and ensuring that it was a BC Native program. Near the end of the interview, Robert Sterling summarized key points and made very positive comments about the work I had been doing in Native education all across Canada. I felt that, all in all, I had left a good impression.

The university year began in July. Not long after the interview, I received a letter offering me the job. I struggled long and hard about whether to accept or not. By then, my mother was diagnosed with terminal cancer and the family was told that she would only live six months to a year. I had no choice but to decline the offer. I had to stay in Winnipeg to help take care of her. The dean called after receiving my letter declining the job offer. I knew that a personal friend of mine, a wonderful Ojibway woman from Manitoulin Island, had also been interviewed and had made a good impression. I urged him to hire her; I felt she would do a great job. I never did learn whether they made her the offer or not.

A few days later, I had a call from the NITEP supervisor to say that she was coming to Winnipeg to see me. I could not figure out why she would be coming when I had declined the job. She came to tell me that the university was willing to wait for me if I would agree to take the job later when I was able to leave Winnipeg. It was still a difficult decision because it meant that I would go after my mother was gone. Though the doctor had said that she would not live long, one always lives in hope of a miracle. The supervisor was very persuasive and we made an agreement; the job would be held for me until I was able to move to Vancouver. It was kept quiet because it was sensitive both for the university and me. Art More returned from his sabbatical leave and became the pro tem NITEP supervisor. He called me and asked if I would be interested in some part-time work. He asked me to teach two Native Studies courses at their NITEP field centres in Kamloops and North Vancouver. They were the only two centres operating, where at one time there had been five. I later learned that this was one of the concerns that the advisory committee had, and they felt that the problem might be better addressed by a Native supervisor. Further to that, he asked if I could spend some time at the university working with him on NITEP. I assumed this was in preparation for my work later on. In all, it was a commitment of one week per month. I accepted. It would become part of my contract work.

Earlier in the year, I had been invited to be the guest speaker at a series of conferences being held in four areas around BC, sponsored by the Ministry of Education. Peg Klesner was working as a consultant for the provincial ministry. I had known Peg since her days in Manitoba as a language arts specialist working for Indian Affairs. She had recommended to her boss that I be invited to be the keynote speaker for a series of Indian education conferences. The theme of the series of conferences was "Communication—The Vital Link." My main message was that parents are the vital link to improving Native education. I spoke of how our people were historically excluded from having any say in their children's education and how, through the policy of Indian Control of Indian Education, all that could now change—and must change if we were to make progress.

Our first conference was held in Vernon, the second in Williams Lake in the BC interior, and our third in Prince Rupert. What a time we had getting to Prince Rupert. We went to the airport to catch our plane and were there in plenty of time. Peg decided she wanted to have a pop, so we looked for one. When we went to board our plane, we were told that our seats had been given away because we were late. I guess we were cutting it a little closer than we realized. We tried to convince them that we had a conference to speak at the next morning and had to get there. No amount of talking would help. Peg's boss offered to give me his seat, but I declined because I felt he had to be there to open the conference. Then we began our search for an alternate way to get to Prince Rupert. All we could get was a flight near midnight to Prince George. From there we would rent a car and drive to Prince Rupert, 700 kilometres away. On top of it all, it had been raining, and as it was winter and cold, the highway was slippery in some areas. Peg had to drive all the way, as I was not used to driving in mountainous areas. I kept wide awake, though, trying to keep Peg going, as we were both very tired. We did not arrive in Prince Rupert until about 6:00 a.m. There was no time to have even a short nap. We showered and got ready for the conference. I was the keynote speaker, and Peg was to introduce me. She told the audience about our trip and we received thunderous applause.

Our last conference was in Victoria. We had no trouble getting there. All the conferences were well attended, and I met many people. I saw much of BC during that time and loved the beauty of the province. I did not know then that this province would become my home for almost twenty years.

I was to begin my work with NITEP in September 1980, teaching Native Studies courses in two centres and spending some time on campus assisting Art More. My mother's health was deteriorating. In August, I drove to Calgary to meet Don, the handsome Cree fellow who had captured my heart back in the 1950s, and who was back in my life. We had planned a two-week holiday in and around the Okanagan.

I met his plane and we went to dinner, and then to the Ambassador Hotel, where I had checked in earlier in the day. We had planned to take in the Indian Ecumenical Conference being held in Morley, Alberta. We headed there the next day. This was a popular conference that was national—in fact, international, since people came from other countries. We attended a few sessions. When night came, we joined others in a teepee that was for visitors. We did have sleeping bags along, but found that sleeping on the ground was very uncomfortable, so we moved on the next day.

Each evening, I would call my sister to see how Mom was doing. I knew it was not right for me to be away at this time, but I wanted to be with Don. I was somewhat troubled about this throughout our time together. We ventured on to Golden, BC. I had previously arranged to meet my cousin Patti and her husband in Golden at a certain motel. They were from Thunder Bay, on a holiday in BC. We met and had a lovely dinner together. They were going to stop to see Mom on their way through Winnipeg. Don and I continued on to the Okanagan. The beauty was overwhelming, but my conscience was bothering me. I knew I should be home with my mother. Finally, after about a week, I told Don that I had better return to Winnipeg. We drove together back to Calgary, and I saw him off on his plane. I returned to Winnipeg. My mother was so happy to see me. She said she had missed me. It was good to be home with her. I probably had told her that I was on a work assignment.

Shortly after I returned, we had to take her to the Winnipeg Health Sciences Centre. She would pass away two weeks later. It was difficult watching our mother fighting for her life. She did not want to die. I guess no one really ever wants to die. She was sixty-seven years old at the time of her death. Now that I am in my seventies, I realize that she did die young.

During the time that my mother was in the hospital, Darlene and I took turns being with her as much as possible. Mary Ann came now and then. We especially wanted to be there at mealtimes, as it became obvious that she could not feed herself. My mother never spoke of her cancer or about her impending death. It was as if she did not know what was happening to her. We didn't press her on it since we were probably just as glad that she didn't seem to want to talk about it. It was too hard to think about. I believe that we were all in denial. From the time that she came to Winnipeg not long after my father's death, she did not want us to say anything to anyone on the reserve about her deteriorating health. I found out later that the people at home just thought that it was because of my father's death that she decided to move to Winnipeg. Given a choice, she would not have left Fisher River. At the time, we all wanted to believe that she would return. When she had to go to the hospital, I did tell some people at Fisher River that she was very ill. A number of people came by to see her. A couple of days before she died she was not always conscious. Jim McKay, a wonderful friend and a relative, came by the evening before she passed away. I told him that she would not likely know him. He spent time in prayer with her. When he came out of her room, he told us that she knew him and had spoken to him. He said she was ready to go. My mother was a strong Christian. She prayed hard for her healing. I know she believed that she would be reunited with her loved ones who had gone before.

She passed away at 6 a.m. on September 18, just ten months after my father. She died at the Princess Elizabeth Hospital, which is a palliative care hospital where she had been moved against the family's wishes on the evening of September 17. My sisters and I had difficulty finding the place. When we did, they were getting her settled. She was not conscious and never regained consciousness. She was in a room with another woman, and it was getting late. No one really spoke to us, though we tried to find out what was going on. Then we left her and returned to our homes. We must have thought that she would remain as she was for a few days since they thought she was well enough to move to palliative care. I have yet to forgive myself for not keeping vigil beside her that night. I was living in my trailer at the time; Darlene and Reggie were on Smithfield, where my mom had lived; and Mary Ann was in East Kildonan. It was very early on the morning of the 18th that I received a call from the Princess Elizabeth Hospital to tell me that our mother was getting weaker and that we should come. I called my sisters and quickly got ready; I picked up Darlene and Reggie. Mary Ann was driven over by her partner, Earl. We weren't there very long before my mother took her last breath. She had waited for us; we had a chance to kiss her and say a few parting words, though she was not conscious. Darlene called a pastor of the Evangelical faith. He came with his wife and had a prayer with us.

I have no idea why we did not contact my Uncle Jim to tell him that she was terminally ill. He and my mother were very close since they had been in foster care in the same home at Fisher River, and when they were adults they lived with my grandmother, Mary Ann, in the family home. When I called my uncle that morning to tell him she had passed away he was very sad and cried. We called our relatives on the reserve and planned to return to Fisher River for her funeral. Many people came to the wakes that were held two nights prior to the funeral. My mother was a good citizen of the reserve and a staunch Christian who believed in talking to those who were having problems in their lives, particularly those who had problems with alcohol. She and my dad ministered to the sick and lonely. They were called to people's homes to bless new homes or for any number of reasons. They were very highly respected. My mother could play the organ, piano, and the piano accordion, all by ear. If someone requested a song or hymn she did not know, she would say, "Hum it for me," then would pick up the tune and play. My mother was the organist at the United Church for many years when I was growing up. My dad was also a musician, and had played the fiddle at dances in his younger days. After his conversion to Christianity, he played in church and at any time they gathered to worship. Both of my parents helped wherever they were called, including in the United, Pentecostal, Apostolic churches and the Mennonite Church in Dallas, a small neighbouring village.

Sometimes they would go to services at various reserves around the province. They even went to Minneapolis and other places in the States. At home, they spent many hours playing hymns together, making tapes. When tape recorders came out my mother always had one with her at services. She would tape the whole service and she would send it to me. One was of a dad taking a service on Mother's Day. For my birthday, she sent me tapes of them singing hymns and choruses. They sang together beautifully. I still have these tapes and listen to them on occasion, thirty years after their deaths. My parents were an inspiration and certainly a loss to the community.

For my mother's funeral, Darlene and I prepared a eulogy. Pamela, Darlene's little girl who was ten years old at the time, saw us writing something so she started to write as well. Later, I asked her what she had written. It was a very moving letter to her grandpa and grandma, telling how much she missed him and how nice it must be for them to be together. She planned to put it in the casket for Mom to take to Dad. Darlene and I asked her if we could read her letter in the church. None of us felt we could read the letter without totally breaking down. My brother-in-law Bill said that he would do it. When it was time to read the letter, he asked Pam to go to the front with him. She did. He had her stand in front of him. He explained how the letter came to be and he read it, and even he could hardly get through it. Pam just stood there with tears in her eyes. You could have heard a pin drop during the reading. We put the letter in the casket, but kept a copy of it. It read:

Dear Grannie and Grandpa,

People say you are dead but it will only make me shed tears in bed. Grannie, I will do everything you would have wanted me to do. I will do it to please you. I will miss you and grandpa up there in the air and lonely old me down here on the ground. Grannie, I know you must be glad because you are up there with your wonderful husband, my wonderful grandpa and besides that you didn't have to suffer very long. I miss you Grannie. Grannie, you are the best Grannie I ever knew. I love you, the same with you Grandpa.

Yours truly,

Pamela Kirkness, your granddaughter who will never
forget you and wishes to be with you because she
loves and wishes to be with you but she can't.

P.S. It won't be the same without you two here to pray for us; but
you still will because you are in heaven. Wish me good luck in
school please. I love you. Love is what keeps our family together.

Losing my mother was probably the most difficult thing I have had to face.
I loved my dad, who was so good to me, but somehow it was different losing
my mother. When I was younger, I felt that my mother resented me and questioned whether she did love me. I was her child born out of wedlock, which
likely had a great effect on her. She was always very hard on me as a child. I
left home at the age of fifteen for high school in Teulon and only returned for
summer holidays. Reggie was born in December 18 of 1950; I left the next
September. My mother dearly loved him, as he was the boy she kept hoping
for. After I became a teacher, I helped my family out as much as I could.

During my first years of teaching, I paid to have electricity hooked up to
our house that my dad had built in 1948. Later, after they got a new house
from the band, I put in running water for them. No one else but the store and
church manse had running water at the time. Later, I got them a new electric
stove and fridge. I provided cars for my dad. The first car he used was one I
had when I left for Norway House (it was a fly-in community at the time,
and there were no cars there). He quickly learned how to drive, and it wasn't
hard to get licences in those days in the small towns. The next car was a black
car that I bought from my friend Colin Wasacase. It was quite sleek, and an
automatic. My dad loved that car, but one winter it burned in a makeshift
slab lumber garage that he built. I can't remember if he got another from
the insurance company or not. Anyway, the last car I bought him was sort of
turquoise, in excellent shape. The day I brought it home, he cried. He was a
diabetic and I hadn't realized that his eyesight had deteriorated so much that
driving was almost impossible for him. I believe I provided them with these
comforts because I could, and I think I did it, especially for my dad, to thank
him for being such a good father to me. It was clear that my gifts meant much

more to him than to my mother. However, as Mom got older, I knew that she truly did love me. She would hug me for a long time when I was leaving from one of my brief visits. She wrote to me faithfully and I do know that I was constantly in their prayers.

When my Uncle Jim died a few years later of cancer at the age of seventy-seven, I felt truly alone. I knew that he was my closest living blood relative. All my mother's siblings were gone. The only blood relatives left were my cousins on my mother's side, but the Kirkness side remains like blood relatives, even to this day.

I was to begin my part-time contract with NITEP in September when university classes started. Since my mother was so weak at the time and died on the 18th, I did not begin the job until October. I would fly to Calgary and then directly to Kamloops on Sundays and teach at the Kamloops NITEP Centre on Mondays. In the first term, I taught a course on the history of Native peoples in Canada, and in the second term I taught about the history of Native education in Canada. I enjoyed being a classroom teacher once again. Except for one course that I taught in a northern Manitoba community for the Brandon University Northern Teacher Education Program, teaching adults was a new experience for me. Most of the students in the NITEP program in the early years were people who had dropped out of high school and were entering under the mature student category. Some had been teacher's aides for a number of years. Several were married with children. There were always more women than men in the program. I found the students very different from the students in northern Manitoba. They were not shy; they asked a lot of questions, offered opinions, and even challenged me on some issues. While this was uncomfortable at times, I liked the interchange. On the whole, they were very bright and had no trouble with the coursework and assignments. I was very strict about assignment completion dates. They had to have very good reasons for any extensions.

One thing I noticed when I arrived in BC was that the students seldom referred to their tribal affiliation. They merely identified as Indian. For me, number one was that I was Cree. I spoke proudly about it and encouraged them to do the same. It was something I discussed in my Native Studies courses. The students would, lightheartedly, tease me and say, "two is company and Cree is a crowd." We had a friendly, yet serious relationship. I was Verna to everyone. Over time, we had Haida, Salish, Squamish, Tsimshian, Carrier, Heiltsuk, Gitksan, Nisga'a, Shuswap, and many other nations represented in our program. No longer were they merely Indian.

Field centres usually had a coordinator and a secretary. The coordinator had to be a jack of all trades, arranging timetables to suit the professors' schedules, driving professors to and from their hotels, and even giving them a lift in the morning, and acting as counsellors and tutors, though they sometimes hired someone to help with tutoring. The coordinator's job required a real commitment; they were virtually on call twenty-four hours a day.

At the end of the day, I would fly to Vancouver to begin teaching the next morning at the North Vancouver NITEP Centre. I didn't stay at a hotel when I was in Vancouver, as my long-time friend and colleague Peg Klesner, who lived in Deep Cove, invited me to stay at her home. We had a lot of good times to talk about when I stayed with her and her friend, Signey. It was very helpful to be with a friend in those times shortly after my mother's death. Peg knew my family, as she had visited our home on a number of occasions. On her last visit to Fisher River she was by then living in Vancouver, so she brought with her a BC salmon. My mother was already ill, but looking forward to her first taste of real BC salmon. Peg and I were in the kitchen, preparing the salmon. She put raw onions as a stuffing and wanted to put some vermouth in the fish to give it taste and to keep it from drying. My mother did not believe in drinking alcohol. Every time Peg went to put vermouth in the fish, my young niece, Gloria, would pop into the kitchen. We thought my mother would not eat the fish if she knew there was alcohol in it. We knew Gloria would tell if she saw what Peg was doing. I guess we were assuming that Gloria knew what vermouth was. We didn't want to take a chance. Finally, the deed was done, and we had a lovely dinner of baked BC salmon.

After teaching in Kamloops and North Vancouver, I spent the remainder of the week working with Art More on campus. I learned how the program worked and assisted wherever possible. I spent time thinking of ways that NITEP could be expanded, since it now had only two centres, down from five. Surely, there were not yet enough Native teachers in BC to meet the need. I thought that we should engage in a process that would involve all people connected to NITEP. I spoke to Art about it, and we began our plans to hold a NITEP Think-In workshop in February. I suggested that we hire Clive Linklater, an expert on structured experiential learning, with whom I had led workshops all across Canada, to conduct the workshop with my assistance. Clive agreed to help, and came to Vancouver for a planning session. Manning Park, about 100 kilometres from Vancouver, was chosen as the site for the workshop. It was important to get the participants away to avoid any distractions from their places of work. Among the participants were Art More and the office staff, including the financial clerk and the secretary; the field centre coordinators; a student representative from each centre and from years three and four from campus; members of the advisory committee; and sponsor teachers—in all, about forty participants. Sponsor teachers were those who had NITEP students practice teaching in their schools. We planned a two-and-a-half-day workshop. The week of the workshop, Clive informed us that he was unable to keep his commitment with us. This made me very nervous because now I was fully in charge. I was familiar with the structured experiences we were going to use to involve every participant, but I was a bit unsure of the processing stage that Clive was so good at. I suggested that we ask Joe Handley, who was now working in Yellowknife, to come and assist me. He did not know about our style of workshop, but having him there gave me confidence. Later, Joe would say, "I got very good at mounting charts on the wall with masking tape."

The workshop of three three-hour blocks a day went very well. One of the main objectives was to make long-term and short-term goals for NITEP. One goal identified was to have a Native dean of education. This was light-hearted, as some ideas were. However, it was not as far-fetched as one might think. Today, Dr. Jo-ann Archibald of the BC Stó:lō Nation is an associate dean of Aboriginal education. It might have taken nearly thirty years, but it happened. One significant point that was negotiated by the students was to have representation on the NITEP advisory committee from each field centre and from years three and four on campus. The students won their case, and they have had representation on the advisory committee ever since.

On April 1, 1981, I officially took over as the supervisor of NITEP, the first Native person to hold the job. I took the job at the rank of assistant professor, which I had been prompted to insist on by Bruce Sealey. Unlike me, he was well versed in how universities worked. I had asked for a certain salary, which was also granted. I agreed to a three-year contract.

Before I left Winnipeg, I purchased some new furniture because I was told that it was very expensive in Vancouver. My first apartment was on West 5th in Kitsilano, a convenient location for going back and forth to UBC. When my furniture arrived, the movers were unable to get my long chesterfield into the elevator. They had to hoist it up on the outside of the building on to the balcony five floors up. I suppose they had to do the same thing when I left. I enjoyed the place, which had a great view of English Bay. When you live in Vancouver, a view becomes very important. I don't suppose I would have left the place if it weren't for my nephew, David. Before my mother died she had asked me to look after David, my sister Mary Ann's son, whom my parents raised since he was two years old. When my mother passed away, he was eighteen, having just completed grade twelve at Charles Sinclair School at Fisher River. The year of my mother's death, David stayed with my brother at my parents' home in Fisher River. He wanted to upgrade his grade twelve to a university entrance level required for the training he wanted to pursue. My second year in Vancouver, I decided to have him come to live with me so he could attend a college to complete his grade twelve. After a few months with the two of us in a one-bedroom apartment, I decided to look for a two-bedroom place. I didn't think it was right for David to be sleeping on a foam mattress in the living room, though he didn't seem to mind. I found a house on West 8th Avenue, even closer to UBC than I was before. I rented the top half of a duplex.

Things seemed to go well for a time with David. He got a paper route and would be out by 5 a.m., delivering papers in the West End. I bought him a bike to help in his paper route. I usually had to wake him up: being a teenager, he liked his sleep. His schoolwork seemed to be going well. He showed me some papers that indicated he was making good progress. When summer came, I sent him to Cedar Cove to work for Jim. When he returned he seemed to have lost interest in school. It came to a point when I realized this was not working out. I had no choice but to send him home to Fisher River.

I still wonder today if I could have done things differently to help David make a productive life for himself. In later years, he would tell me that he was sorry that he didn't take advantage of the time he was with me in Vancouver.

I liked my place on West 8th, which was within short walking distance of Jericho Beach. At the apartment on West 5th, I was just three blocks from Kitsilano Beach. I loved walking to the beach and sitting by the water, listening to the waves lap up against the shore. It reminded me of the days when we would go out on lake with my dad to his fishing camp at Black Fox on Lake Winnipeg. The house on West 8th had a large backyard with an apple tree. The first couple of years that I lived there I made a lot of applesauce. I had never canned food before, but I enjoyed this. I also learned to can salmon. When Jo-ann Archibald still lived in Chilliwack she would invite one of our colleagues, Val Friesen, and me to go to her place on a Saturday to can fish. We cut the fish a certain way and stuffed it into pint jars that we had sterilized, added just a bit of salt and nothing else, and put the jars in a big boiler of water on the stove to cook slowly. It is still the best salmon I have ever eaten—except, of course, for the salmon prepared by other Native people who do it in a similar way. Years later, I am still treated to jarred salmon from my friends in BC.

At the university, our headquarters was in an old army hut. These were to be temporary housing for programs after the huts were no longer needed by the army. In 1981, they were still in use at UBC, though they were slowly being replaced by permanent buildings. The NITEP Centre was in a hut that had been remodelled to accommodate the program. It had a main office for the secretary and the financial clerk, and separate offices for the supervisor, the assistant to the supervisor, the on-campus coordinator, and the counsellor. There were another couple of offices and a student lounge complete with chesterfields and tables to be used by the students. The lounge was the hub of the centre. Students enjoyed having this space to meet, have lunch, work on assignments together, hold meetings, and have visitors. It was their home away from home. After observing how important this lounge was for our students, I became a strong advocate for having universities and colleges designate space for Native students to gather. The NITEP Centre also had space for a small library with a very scant collection. NITEP was to occupy this space until 1993, when we moved into our new building, the Longhouse.

Besides the staff in the NITEP hut we had coordinators and secretaries at each field centre. Faye Halls was the secretary at the North Van Centre. After she met me, she told her dad about me. It turned out her father was Simon Baker, a prominent citizen of the Squamish Nation, known as Chief Simon Baker, and a respected spokesman of Native people and non-Native people alike. I had met him ten years earlier at a national cultural conference in Ottawa organized by Dr. Ahab Spence, who was the director of the Cultural Section with the Department of Indian Affairs. I had been impressed with Simon's contribution to the discussion as he was with my comments. We got to visiting and sharing our experiences and thoughts about culture. That was during my time with the Manitoba Indian Brotherhood in the early 1970s. I was happy to see him again when he came to greet me at the North Vancouver Centre. It was a fortuitous meeting, as he would become a staunch supporter of my work at UBC. Simon would be the first of three Elders who would advise and sustain me while I was at UBC. I became very close to Simon's whole family. One day, Simon asked me if I would write his life story. After much consideration, I decided to do it. He recorded much of his story, and after I transcribed what he had taped and spent hours interviewing him, the theme became very clear to me—he was an ambassador of his own culture and of the human spirit. I borrowed this appropriate description of him from the Sechelt Nation when they honoured him for his contribution to the advancement of their nation.

Having taken over the job of supervisor, I set out to follow the directions I received during my interview, one of which was to increase the number of BC Native people on staff in the program. One of the first things I did was to hire Jo-ann Archibald to organize a Native Awareness Day on campus and to assist the program in other ways. In 1981, the first Native Awareness Day was held at UBC. We even had a marching band from the St. Mary's Residential School. At the same time, we held an open house at the NITEP hut so visitors could see where Native students hung out. It was a successful event and helped to make NITEP more visible.

The next year, we reopened a NITEP field centre in Chilliwalk. We held a competition for a coordinator. Jo-ann applied at my urging, and she got the job. That was the beginning of a long and fruitful career for Jo-ann with the University of British Columbia, where she remains to this day.

A huge concern that was expressed during my job interviews and again at the Think-In workshop at Manning Park was the need to increase the number of NITEP centres. I criss-crossed the province speaking about NITEP, talked about establishing field centres, and met with potential students. I was fortunate that Val Friesen was my assistant. He was a tireless worker who was totally committed to NITEP. He knew the program well, as he had been with it almost since its inception. He was more than capable of holding the fort while I travelled throughout the province scouting for students to determine where we could establish centres. There had previously been a centre at Williams Lake. Alan Haig-Brown, the education coordinator for the Williams Lake School District, felt there were enough potential candidates in the area to reopen a centre. I went to spend a few days with him, and he took me to a number of surrounding Native Indian communities. I spoke to several people, mostly former students who had dropped out of school or had a partial high-school education. They would be eligible to enroll in NITEP through the mature student category that was open to all students. Alan knew which students would make good candidates as he had worked and lived in the area for many years. I recall one particular incident where we were going by a school when we saw a woman lying on the lawn. Alan said that I should get out of the truck and go and talk to her about NITEP. She was practically asleep when I got to her. She was waiting for her children to come out of school. I talked to her and asked if she might be interested in becoming a teacher. She said she would think about it. Adeline and I would later laugh about her recruitment on the lawn of the school. She did extremely well in NITEP and earned the reputation of being one of the top-notch teachers in the province. I recruited other students who were sitting on an old truck outside a restaurant. There were no holds barred in my recruitment methods. The magic number of potential candidates to open a centre in a town was fifteen. We opened a centre at Williams Lake that next fall.

During that first year with NITEP, I attended an international conference in Santa Fe, New Mexico. There I met Catherine McKinnon, who was with the Donner Canadian Foundation. This meeting would have a profound effect on the future of my work at UBC. My purpose in attending various conferences was to give papers on NITEP as a model for teacher education for Native people. I pointed out the features that made NITEP a successful model. The field centre concept was significant in that it allowed students to remain closer to home to attend classes in a setting that was not as intimidating as a huge university like UBC. They spent their first two years at a field centre, taking arts courses that included two Native Studies courses. In addition, they spent time in classrooms during the first semester, getting first-hand experience in teaching. It was felt that this would enable the students to find out early whether or not teaching was for them. (The so-called regular program of teacher education at UBC adopted this practice several years later when revamping their program. Prior to this, the "regular" students did not get into the classrooms until their last year of training.) We encouraged cooperation among our students rather than competition, a traditional value of our people. NITEP was a cohort model, one that we would later emulate for programs in other areas. In the case of NITEP, the cohort is made up of Aboriginal students who share common backgrounds and experiences and can provide peer cooperation and support to each other.

Catherine McKinnon was very interested in what we were doing at UBC and told me that I should apply to the Donner Canadian Foundation if I needed money to support NITEP. One of the attractions I had to NITEP when I considered taking the job was UBC's financial commitment to the program. In my experience, I found most universities who planned to serve the Native population sought and received funding from the Department of Indian Affairs. In fact, UBC was the only university I knew of that funded its own program. This, to me, was a sign of real commitment. However, with the budget available to us at the time, I realized it would be difficult to open new centres, even though this was the desired direction. I was in Ottawa for a meeting, staying at Jim's, when I remembered what Catherine McKinnon had said and decided to ask the Donner Foundation to assist us with funding so we could increase our number of centres. It was before the days of easy access to computers. I don't know why I didn't wait until I got back to Vancouver to send a properly typewritten letter to the foundation. Jim did not have a typewriter or computer, so I wrote a three-page handwritten letter expressing UBC's need to expand the NITEP program. I addressed the letter to the director, Mr. Don Rickles. I guess that got their attention at the foundation. It certainly showed that I did not know who Don Rickles was, though the name was somewhat familiar. I received a response from Don Rickerd, asking me to submit a proposal. Yes, his last name was Rickerd. The foundation agreed to give us $300,000 over three years. Well, this certainly impressed the UBC establishment. Then I decided to apply for funding from the Department of Indian Affairs, which was a change from my earlier thinking. Now, I felt that UBC should get a share of the monies being provided to other universities for their teacher education programs. We began receiving funding from DIA. The two sources of funding substantially increased the NITEP budget, and we were able to establish new centres.

During my three years of being directly in charge of NITEP, the highest number of NITEP centres we had was seven and a half. We had the two original centres in Kamloops and North Vancouver; we reopened centres in Chilliwack and Williams Lake; and new centres were opened in Victoria, Hazelton, and Vancouver East, with a half-time centre in Bella Coola. I travelled frequently to the field centres. I enjoyed being with the students and encouraging them to be positive about their impending move to the campus to complete their degrees. When I returned from a Kamloops visit, I would tell the Vancouver staff that Kamloops was the best centre. Then upon returning from Hazelton, I told them it had to be the best centre. And so it went as I visited each place. I loved it!

I held coordinators' meetings on campus once a month. We would have day-long meetings because it was my policy to have open communication, not only with the coordinators, but also with our on-campus staff and students. I tried to involve them in the ongoing direction of the program. At the end of our coordinators' meetings, all the staff would get together for dinner, usually at someone's home. Sheila Te Hennepe, our on-campus counsellor, had a house near campus and so we met there several times, often making it a potluck meal. On one occasion, Dana, the coordinator for the Vancouver East

Centre, invited us to the house he was renting in North Vancouver. He told us to bring our bathing suits because he had a hot tub. It was a lovely place surrounded by beautiful flowers and trees. It wasn't long before the men on staff—Dana, Val, Terry, and Gus—were in the hot tub. I put on my bathing suit and found that none of the other women wanted to go in. That was fine; I went on my own. What I didn't realize was that the fellows were in the nude. When I got there they were chuckling and all turned toward the wall of the tub. When I knew what was going on, I was not going to back down, but got in the tub with them, keeping my eyes up. One by one they got out. Later they told the others that "they hide nothing from their supervisor." It was funny!

Each year there were Canadian Indian Teacher Education Programs (CITEP) conferences that brought together people involved in Native teacher education programs across the country. In February of 1981, just before I joined NITEP on a full-time basis, I was asked to be the keynote speaker for the CITEP conference being hosted at UBC by NITEP. I chose as my topic "Why TEP?" (Teacher Education Programs). As might be expected, the Native teacher education programs emerging across the country were suspect and said to be watered-down teacher education programs. In my address, I argued that, to the contrary, the programs were not special programs but superior programs intended to better prepare our teachers for their work in Native schools. The programs operated on the principle that those trained in these programs were likely to return to teach in their home communities, though with their Bachelor of Education degrees they could teach anywhere in the province. This was a theme I continued to develop during my time with NITEP. I wanted our graduates to be ready with a reply if and whenever they met skeptics who questioned their credentials. I remember being asked at a meeting of non-Native colleagues how long we were going to need to have programs like NITEP. My response was, "Until the regular program provides the kind of teacher education that will assist our students to be better teachers in their communities." It is now 2013, and NITEP still exists as do other similar programs at other universities. Clearly universities have not taken up the challenge.

I never felt restricted in any way by senior administration. My immediate superior was the dean of education, who was Dr. Roy Bentley when I arrived there. He left soon after, and Dr. Dan Birch became the new dean. I had the privilege of meeting Dan and his wife Arlene before he took over. He had been a vice-president at Simon Fraser University when Peg Klesner was on staff there. Peg invited the Birches and me to go sailing with her. I found out that Dan had been behind the Native teacher education program that Simon Fraser University had established at Mount Currie reserve. He seemed very interested in Native education. Well, I was certainly pleased when he took the job at UBC.

The assistant to the dean, Dr. Murray Elliot, was a member of the NITEP advisory committee that oversaw the NITEP program and the body to whom I reported. The minutes of our meetings were forwarded to the dean. I can remember times when Murray would tell us that we might have difficulty getting approval for certain things we were discussing. I believe that he was the reason that we felt no interference from the powers that be. I always informed the advisory committee members about what I was doing and sought their approval before making any major decisions. I know they appreciated that and knew that they were playing a significant role as a committee.

The dean was pleased with my work in NITEP. Not only did I increase the number of centres, but I also brought in a lot of money. The number of graduates increased year by year. The first year I was there, having just arrived on April 1, 1981, we had three graduates. It was a tradition in NITEP to have a separate celebration besides the university's convocation ceremony where students were awarded their degrees. The separate celebration enabled the students to invite their families to celebrate with them. As the supervisor, I was expected to emcee the occasion. I followed past tradition: there was a guest speaker and a celebratory toast with real champagne. In 1982, the *Vancouver Sun* was invited to our slightly bigger grad, now moved to the Scarf Theatre, and on the front page appeared the nine graduates with glasses of champagne held high in celebration. I don't remember the circumstances surrounding the elimination of this practice, but it was discontinued, likely because this was not the image we wanted to project of our graduates, who were sure to be seen as role models. In 1983, we had to rent the Totem Park ballroom because our number of graduates was increasing. This venue continued to be used until 1993, when we moved into the Longhouse and had our own Great Hall called Sty-Wet-Tan (Spirit of the West Wind) for our celebrations. The dean used to joke about our continued growth and would say that before long we would be renting BC Place stadium.

The number of Native people on staff was increasing. When one of the faculty or staff members resigned, I made every effort to attract Native candidates to replace them. Over time, most of the coordinators were Native, several of whom were NITEP graduates. We were growing!

We started a newsletter based on a recommendation at our first annual Think-In workshop. It was called the *NITEP News*, another tradition that has stood the test of time. It is now published annually and is a great vehicle to inform people about NITEP. During my three years with NITEP, we continued to have our annual Think-Ins and invited the dean as well. He did come and spent at least a day with us. We held the first one at Manning Park, another on Whidbey Island, and the third was at the old St. Mary's Residential School. We had a strange experience at St. Mary's. Several people had difficulty sleeping and felt distressed. The school had closed as a residential school only a year earlier. Several of the participants had been to school there and had mixed memories about their experiences. We persevered and suggested to those in charge of the place to have it blessed by the Elders.

Another significant advance was the development of the NITEP library. The group of Native students who lobbied for NITEP in the early seventies had also been responsible for establishing the Native Education Resource Centre. The centre had since closed and boxes of books and materials on Native people had been stored away. I decided to prepare a funding proposal to build up the library, beginning with the materials that were in storage. I applied to the H.R. McMillan Foundation, which I learned had an interest in libraries, and, to my delight, the foundation granted us $100,000. I would later receive more money from them. I hired on contract the only Native person I knew of who had a master's degree in library science to develop our library. Gene Joseph of the Wet'suwet'en Nation is well-known today as the person who developed the library, which was later housed in a separate building, part of the Longhouse complex, known as X̱wi7x̱wa Library. X̱wi7x̱wa (pronounced whei-wha) means "echo" in the Squamish language. The name was given by Chief Simon Baker. He chose that name as echo was a means of communication among their people in the early days. After I retired, I was invited to chair an event at the Longhouse to honour Gene Joseph, who was having a library scholarship named after her. It was a wonderful occasion. As a joke, I had a lovely 6 x 9 photo of Gene framed. I said I would auction off the photo, and the proceeds would go to Gene's new scholarship fund. Of course, she was embarrassed by this surprise auction but took it in good stride, and it made for a lot of laughter as the price increased dollar by dollar. At that event, Gene gave away lovely framed prints done by Don Yeomans, a Haida/Métis artist, a protegé of her partner Bud Mintz. Mine still hangs in my home in Winnipeg.

Very early on, probably in my second year, Dr. Birch approached me to apply for tenure. I had never given this a thought since I saw my job as ending with my three-year contract. Granted, I was well-established in Vancouver and loved the city and the university. The job was exactly the challenge I needed at the age of forty-five, with the privilege of a wide experience in Native education behind me, and a university ready to do more to serve the Native people. I knew it was quite unusual for a person holding a Master of Education degree to even think of being considered for tenure. This was the sacred domain of those with PhDs. Dan informed me that they could not extend my contract, as the regulations allowed for a maximum of three years for a contract. He tried to impress upon me that I should continue in my employment with UBC, and to do that I would have to get on the tenure track. I told him that tenure would make no difference to me; I would leave whenever I wanted to, regardless of a "secured" position. Dan was very persuasive, and I agreed to pursue tenure. Tenure is a long process that takes some people years to attain, and some never make it.

I believe you are allowed up to seven years to obtain tenure. You were assessed by your teaching, which I had done with NITEP before I actually joined the program full-time. I would later be assessed on my teaching at the graduate level when I taught a couple of courses in the Ts"kel (Golden Eagle) program. What was important to the university was research, teaching, and community service. I was to compile a portfolio of my research that amounted to the papers I had given over the years beginning in 1964. I had a number of articles published in journals, several of which were refereed journals that counted toward tenure. I had co-edited a resource book entitled

Indians Without Tipis and wrote a book for Grolier of Canada called *Indians of the Plains*, which became a grade four social studies textbook. I had written a number of published studies. My community work had always been a strong component of my jobs. I began my tenure-track journey in 1984; in 1990, I received tenure and was promoted to associate professor at the same time.

TS''KEL IS BORN

I loved my work with the Native Teacher Education Program, but in my usual pattern it led to another important development. At one of our graduation celebrations, likely in 1983, we invited as our guest speaker Sharon Mack, a former NITEP graduate. Sharon was teaching in her home community of Bella Coola at the time. It was inspiring to the students to have one of the graduates speak to them about her experiences as a NITEP student and as a teacher. During the course of the event, Sharon mentioned to me that there was a need for further education for the NITEP graduates who were out there teaching because there were opportunities for them to become school principals. I kept thinking about what Sharon had said. I talked about it with Dr. Birch, the dean of education. He was encouraging and suggested that I speak with Dr. Downey, the head of UBC's Administrative, Adult and Higher Education (AAHE) department. We needed to consider a master's degree in educational administration, and AAHE was responsible for the area. I continued to go about my business in NITEP, as there was a lot to attend to in a program that had grown to capacity.

One day, I had a call from Dr. Downey to say that Dean Birch had called to tell him I wanted a meeting with him. I have to thank Dean Birch for forcing the issue. After I had spoken to him about it, I just continued to mull it over in my own mind. Dr. Downey and I met, and I found him to be very enthusiastic about considering what we might do for Native Indians who wanted to get further education to advance in their careers. I told the NITEP advisory committee members about this possibility, and they were very much in favour. I described the proposed program as being somewhat like an extension of NITEP, and, in fact, we determined they would be the advisory committee to the new program as well. We changed the title of the committee to the Native Indian Advisory Committee. This was fitting, as

I was now the director of Native Indian Education and I saw this body as overseeing all of my work. Meetings continued with the planning committee of the AAHE department, and before long we had an outline of what we could do to begin the program. We moved quickly, as I like to do, and with the department and the dean's support we planned to start the program in the fall of 1984, just months after I presented the idea to Dr. Downey. Only one advanced program for Indian leaders existed in Canada at the time, the Brandon University Indian Leadership Development Program (BUILD). The BUILD Program did not continue for very long. Ts"kel continues to be a vibrant program.

I was named to head the program, though, technically, I was the director of Native education. With a $55,500 grant from the Donner Canadian Foundation, we developed the Ts"kel program. The money was used for materials development and for program evaluation. The Donner Canadian Foundation made a valuable contribution to enable the expansion of NITEP, to initiate and develop the Ts"kel program, and later to create and develop the First Nations House of Learning.

And so we began with three students, Shirley Myran from Manitoba; Ethel Gardner, a NITEP graduate who had just completed a Diploma in Creative Writing; and Francis Johnson, also a NITEP graduate, who was teaching in his home community of Alkali Lake. Thus, a master's program in educational administration for Native people was born. We were able to begin this program very quickly; it did not require Senate approval as it was seen as an adaptation of the existing program, not a new one. This was a similar approach to that adopted by NITEP years earlier.

Dr. Downey took great pride in the program and, in 1987, wrote a book entitled *The Story of Ts"kel*, in which he gave a detailed account of the initiation and development of the program. It was interesting that he pointed out an aspect of the program I had not given much thought to, namely, that the infusion of Native Indian students into the department was seen as a mutually advantageous endeavour. For the students, it was an opportunity for advanced study and preparation for leadership positions, and, for the department, an opportunity to integrate into its value system an important but heretofore largely ignored aspect of Canadian culture.

The "regular" master's program had as a prerequisite an introductory three-credit educational administration summer course taught by Dr. Pat Crehan, which served as a screening course for all students pursuing a Master of Educational Administration. Pat was known as an excellent and demanding professor, and no one passed her course without a lot of serious studying. Our three students passed her course, which was the first hurdle.

The Master of Educational Administration required students to complete fifteen units of credit along with a major paper. Typically, full-time students completed the program within two years. The intent of our version of the Ts"kel program, as it came to be known, was to prepare students for work in band schools (Indian-controlled schools), though the degree in no way limited them to these schools. It was Shirley, Ethel, and Francis, our first students, who named the program, *Ts"kel*, which means "golden eagle" in the Halq'emeylem language. NITEP has as its logo the raven that brought light to the world, according to a West Coast legend. These students chose the eagle, as it soars higher than the raven.

In order to bring together the realities of the band school and the views held by Indian educational leaders, it was necessary to adapt some of the courses. I taught a special seminar, Educational Administration (EDM 508), as a foundation course designed to acquaint students with the history of Indian education, the prevailing philosophies of current education leaders, and the historical, legislative, and cultural antecedents of Native Indian education in Canada, with an emphasis on British Columbia. This was an opportunity for students to share their knowledge and experiences of the situation as they knew it. Each student was required to prepare a case study designed to capture the current context of Native Indian education and to analyze the case studies using concepts of educational administration.

We decided that our students would do a two-week field placement, working with school principals, rather than the one week required in the regular master's program. I chose schools with a high Indian enrollment in and around Vancouver. As we anticipated that most of our Ts"kel students would already have taught for a number of years, those who had a band school experience were placed in an urban setting, and if a student was in an urban school, they were required to have a band school experience. Students kept journals and later had an opportunity to discuss their observations in the group. What were the strong points of the way the school was administered? What were the weak points? How would they improve the school if they were in charge?

We adapted the course, Administering a Public School, to become Administering a Band School. The course for public schools had been developed by Professors Walter Hartrick and Shirley Nalevykin, and they headed the development of our adapted course. In order to get current realistic situations, Walter, Shirley, and I visited a number of band schools throughout the province. On these visits, Walter collected data from the principals and administrators, Shirley visited teachers, and I spoke to teachers, particularly Native language teachers and teacher's aides.

After the materials were gathered, the students, along with Shirley and Walter, created a simulation, the Ts''kel community and the Ts''kel Band School. On the day the simulation materials were being used, each student was given an office representing a newly appointed principal. In each office was an in-box and an out-box. The in-box contained the tasks principals typically have to deal with. They began at 9 a.m., as one would on a school day. Several people were identified to play the roles of parent, teacher, child, salesman, etc. They were to make telephone calls to the principals about problems. In the meantime, the principals were trying to prioritize and deal with their in-boxes. It was a pressure-filled morning. Later, the students would analyze their experiences. It was a fun exercise with a lot of learning.

While travelling for the Ts''kel program, Shirley, Water, and I had several harrowing experiences on planes, trains, boats, and automobiles. Shirley and I still talk about these experiences when we get together. On a visit to Mount Currie School, located just north of Whistler, we planned to attend an evening school board meeting. We arrived at Mount Currie near 6:00 p.m. and decided we would not eat until after the meeting, which was to begin an hour later. The meeting started much later once everyone had arrived, and it didn't end until around eleven o'clock. Needless to say, we were famished. We looked for a place to eat and found everything was closed for the night except for the bar at the hotel, which was about to close as well. They didn't carry much in the way of food, so we had only pickled eggs to carry us over until the next day.

We also visited the school in Ahousat, a short distance from Tofino, accessible only by water or plane. It was a lovely drive to Tofino. When we got there, it was very windy. A man from Ahousat was there to meet us by boat. It was a small boat with an outboard motor, and water was splashing in on us because the waves were high. We arrived there a bit wet, but safe. We spent the day working in the school and would leave at the end of the day. The wind continued to blow, and the principal had arranged to have a small plane take us back to Tofino, as it was too rough to go back by boat. Shirley was deathly afraid of flying, as she still is, and usually uses the train for her travels. It took some doing to get us on the little float plane that was bobbing about by the dock. We got off without incident and after a very short but bumpy ride we landed and coasted up to a dock in Tofino. We decided to stop for the night at Long Beach, where we barbequed steaks we had bought in Tofino. We enjoyed a pleasant evening rehashing our ordeal. There were other memorable trips, but through it all we were able to collect the data we required for the course.

The pioneers of the program all graduated by 1986, within two years of its inception. The program was and continues to be highly successful thanks to the calibre of the students, the professors, and the educational administration contingent. While there may have been some skepticism at the beginning, Ts"kel quickly gained a good reputation for its quality.

I think of the Ts"kel program as one of my greatest achievements at UBC. From 1984 to the time I left UBC in 1993, we had twenty master's graduates and another twenty-three were in progress, five of whom graduated with PhDs. In about 1986, we extended the program to include doctoral students. Now headed by a Ts"kel graduate, the program continues to graduate more and more educational leaders that are gainfully employed and are providing tremendous leadership in the Aboriginal community.

In 2008, I was invited to UBC to speak to the Aboriginal doctoral students at their annual seminar. To my joy and surprise, there were 100 doctoral students from the three universities in BC. The vast majority were from UBC. From our modest beginning in 1984 to prepare teachers for educational administration at the master's level, Aboriginal education has grown to include doctoral students in specialized fields of education such as special education and social and educational studies, and to other faculties such as psychology, anthropology, counselling, medicine, agriculture, and commerce. I take great pride in knowing that we planted the seed all that many years ago.

Our flourishing programs provided momentum to expand the opportunities for Aboriginal students and their communities, like a snowball that just keeps getting bigger and bigger as it rolls along. The time was right to move ahead because there was a willing administration, a funding source that was interested in supporting expansion of needed programs, and exciting new program ideas, with a large cohort of Aboriginal students eager to take advantage of higher education. The successes of NITEP, the Ts"kel Graduate Program, and the Native Law Program were the incentive for developments to follow at UBC.

During this time, a momentous historical event was taking place with the passing of Bill C-31 on June 28, 1985. It would amend the Indian Act of 1867 and restore status and membership rights to women who lost it by marrying a non-Indian. My sister Mary Ann had lost her status when she married a German fellow. She had applied and was approved to be reinstated, along with her sons. She called me one day and suggested that I apply for my status. She sent me the appropriate forms and advised me how to get the required live birth record from the Province of Manitoba. Strangely enough, it had never occurred to me to apply for my status. I sent in my application, and in a letter dated April 27, 1988, I was advised that I was now recognized by the Government of Canada as a Status Indian and a member of the Fisher River Band. I was fifty-three years old. While I was not a Bill C-31 applicant, it was this bill that prompted my action. Having status has enabled me to vote in band elections and makes me eligible for non-insured health services and my five-dollar treaty money each year.

THE FIRST NATIONS HOUSE OF LEARNING

Initially, the majority of Native Indian students at the university were in the fields of education or law. As our Native Indian communities were assuming more and more responsibility for managing their own affairs, the demand for more professionals in other fields such as health, agriculture, commerce, and engineering was evident.

When I would talk with Tom Berger, a prominent lawyer and a strong advocate for the rights of Indigenous people, we talked a lot about education. I got to know him through his wife, Beverly, who was the on-campus NITEP coordinator at the time. He was happy to see the NITEP program flourishing. Being a lawyer, he was aware of the Native Law Program, but felt that more could be happening. He cited the growing number of Native Studies departments springing up at various universities across Canada. I shared his concern, but I was already quite overwhelmed with my current responsibilities to act on it—so we continued to talk. Finally, one day we decided it was time to act. I'm not sure I shared with him my misgivings about Native Studies departments at that time. While Native Studies was great in terms of dealing with our legal, economic, and social circumstances, I was afraid that it would become a ghetto for Native students. A second concern I had was about job opportunities for graduates with a Native Studies degree. I had spoken to a number of students with Native Studies degrees and was told they found the job market limited.

I did, however, agree wholeheartedly with Tom that we ought to explore the question of increasing the number of Aboriginal students on campus. I credit Tom Berger with his interest and persistence to grow the university to serve a greater purpose than it was already doing.

It was in 1984 when Tom approached the president of UBC, Dr. George Pedersen, to discuss the matter. Dr. Pedersen's response was positive, and as a first step he struck a committee mandated to advise him on what the university should be doing for First Nations and their communities. Tom and I were appointed co-chairs. The committee, known as the President's Ad Hoc Committee, was comprised of representatives from First Nations communities, UBC faculty, and federal and provincial governments. We held a series of meetings over a period of a few months and tabled our report with the president. The main recommendation was that a First Nations Institute be established to oversee access and support services to encourage more First Nations students to enroll in various faculties at UBC. Rather than creating a Native Studies department, our direction was to ensure that each faculty in the university would address First Nations access and support.

Though the president agreed with the recommendations from the report, his response was very disappointing. He was unable to act on them as the university was facing serious financial cutbacks at the time.

The report remained dormant until 1987, when Dr. David Strangway became president and the financial situation at UBC had improved. Tom always had his ear to the ground, and when he was aware that a new president was to be appointed, he wrote a letter to Dr. Strangway, then a vice-president at the University of Toronto, to tell him about the report that was prepared recommending that the university improve access and support for First Nations.

Much to my surprise and pleasure, Dr. Strangway requested I meet with him on the Friday morning of his first week as president. He wanted me to apprise him of what was currently happening with First Nations at the university. I told him about the success of NITEP, Ts"kel, and the Native Law Program. Then he enquired about the President's Ad Hoc Committee Report and asked whether I thought it was still a good idea to pursue the establishment of a First Nations Institute. I confirmed the serious need to address access and support on-campus because the need for Aboriginal professionals in our communities was becoming more urgent.

I told him about my experience with the Donner Canadian Foundation that had provided grants for the expansion of NITEP and the creation of the Ts"kel graduate program. When the idea for a First Nations Institute arose, I had contacted the foundation to determine if they would be willing, once again, to assist us with a start-up grant. They expressed an interest and advised me to send a proposal for their consideration. Dr. Strangway's response was "Go for it!" That was my green light to get on with the project.

The Donner Canadian Foundation agreed to provide a start-up grant of $300,000 over three years. The foundation wisely included a stipulation that if the programs they supported were successful in their mandate and objectives, the university had to agree to carry on the program with full funding. The university agreed, and funding was in place for three years, from 1987 to 1990. Up to this point, I had brought in a considerable amount of money into the university.

The First Nations House of Learning was to be administered by the President's Office. I had heard rumours that the anthropology department felt that it should be under its jurisdiction, since it was about Indians. I would have fought against that had it become an issue—our program was committed to a present, living movement and resisted being seen as fossils of the past. Being under the President's Office, I was able to ensure that the doors to all faculties and departments were open to us to promote access and support for our students. My immediate superior was the vice-president (academic) and provost, Dr. Dan Birch. Once again, we were working together—this was a great blessing, as he was sensitive to the needs of First Nations people. As a dean, he had encouraged and supported my idea for a graduate program in education for First Nations people and had urged me to work toward tenure. It was a pleasure to meet with him to discuss possibilities, as he was not a person to simply turn down an idea. His approach was more about helping to find ways to accomplish your goals.

An issue arose early on related to the use of the term "institute." The vice-president (research and development) argued that our use of the term did not conform to the functions of the existing institutes at the university. It was apparent that we had to come up with another name. I discussed this issue with the advisory committee, and Joan Ryan, a Gitksan, suggested that we call it the "house of learning," from the Gitksan expression denoting "a place of learning." As we discussed this possibility, we realized that most Aboriginal languages translate references to schools, colleges, or universities as "places where you go to learn." With the concurrence of all parties, the name officially became the "First Nations House of Learning."

We formed a First Nations House of Learning Advisory Committee with a similar composition as that of the President's Ad Hoc Committee, to which we added Elders and students. Tom Berger was named the chair of the committee, and I was seconded, theoretically, on a half-time basis, from the Faculty of Education as the director for a three-year term that turned out to be six years, from 1987 to 1993. I continued to carry my other responsibilities. By this time, I was wearing several hats at UBC—director of Native Indian Education, overseeing NITEP and Native Studies courses, and working with the Ts'kel graduate program. I was also editing an annual issue of the *Canadian Journal of Native Education* as well as participating with the wider Aboriginal community. Meanwhile, I was organizing a World Conference on Aboriginal Education and working with Chief Simon Baker on his memoirs. It was an extremely busy but happy time for me.

Kathy Morven, a very capable young lady, was hired as my secretary. We advertised for an assistant director, and Ethel Gardner was hired. Ethel, a NITEP and Ts"kel graduate, was at the time the head of the Indian Education department at the Saskatchewan Indian Federated College in Regina. She was doing well there, but when the position at the House of Learning came up she applied because her family all lived in and around Vancouver. Later, a coordinator's position was created. Madeleine MacIvor, another graduate of the NITEP and Ts"kel programs, was hired. I strongly advocated during my time at UBC that we should hire our own graduates, and it proved fruitful for us; we formed a strong team. The First Nations Health Care Professions Program, initiated in 1988, became part of the House of Learning until it moved to the Faculty of Medicine (as was the intent from the beginning). The House of Learning staff numbers have not increased substantially over the years. It was never about building a large staff; it was to have the new programs become part of whichever faculty initiated them. The House of Learning was to promote access and support for First Nations students throughout the university and to bring the university and the First Nations community closer together.

This was done in a variety of ways. Much of our first year was spent conducting workshops in First Nations communities to familiarize them with what the university had to offer and to determine their priorities for the kinds of expertise they will require as they move toward self-reliance. In other words, what kinds of jobs should their students be preparing to undertake to serve their communities? After an intense consultation process, Ethel presented her report, which set the direction for the House of Learning. Her recommendations were as follows:

(1) education, emphasizing the need for specific, specialized training for First Nations teachers that included physical education, curriculum development, speech-language pathology, English as a second language, and First Nations languages; (2) health care, with an emphasis on preparing counsellors (family, drug and alcohol, sexual abuse), dentists, and nurses; (3) natural

resource sciences, namely fisheries, forestry, marine biology, and agriculture; (4) commerce and business administration, including band planners and managers; and (5) training for First Nations language teachers, linguists, curriculum developers and translators.

In response, one of the first steps was to create the First Nations Health Care Professions Program. During Angie Todd-Dennis's time as coordinator, she organized a series of workshops with high-school students. She wanted to motivate them to think about their careers, in particular making them aware of the health field. On one occasion, she invited me to conduct a student workshop in a northern town. The workshop was to begin at 9 a.m., but with a storm brewing, several buses were late arriving. When we thought they were all there, we began. More buses arrived, and we had to find a larger room. I believe she expected about forty students and over 100 came. I had a number of activities for them to engage in, which they did with enthusiasm. I had them work in groups; on a flip chart they were to list all the forms of employment that they had in their communities. Then we discussed who held these jobs. Usually, they were people from outside the community. What did they have to do if they were to take over these jobs? What if none of these jobs were of interest to them—what did that mean for their further education? Our aim was to have them think of the choices they would have to make for post-secondary education based on their interests, and taking into consideration whether they saw themselves remaining in their communities or working elsewhere.

The Health Care Professions Program initiated a Summer Science Program in 1988 for grades eight and nine and grades eleven and twelve students, with each group spending one week on campus. Through vetted applications, a number of students from across BC were chosen each year to spend one week on campus engaging in science activities and getting acquainted with the university. A staff consisting of Elders who brought their traditional knowledge related to science, as well as chaperones, science teachers, and professors led the program. Aboriginal speakers were invited to talk about different aspects of science and First Nations cultures. On the final day, parents were invited to listen to the students' presentations. I recall one such evening being hosted by President Strangway at his home. The students (grades eight and nine) who entered the program just days before as shy, quiet students were bubbling over with pride, and all wanted to make a speech. The president was very moved by this, as we all were. We kept in touch with these students, and I was there long enough to see several of those summer science students come to UBC after they graduated from grade twelve. A similar program that was called Synala was initiated for those students interested in the arts.

We used workshops as a way to communicate with potential students in rural and remote areas of BC. We began preparing brochures outlining our mandate and objectives, and we created an annual newsletter. Madeleine was in charge of this area. Meetings were held with various faculties to encourage them to make a commitment to strive toward greater access and support for First Nations students. It took several years to make anything happen in a number of faculties we targeted. It depended very much on the will of the dean. We were breaking new ground and it would take time for the idea to gain support. Subsequent leaders worked on the same principle over the years. As a result, First Nations students are now represented in a wide range of faculties beyond Education and Law, including the faculties of Applied Science, Arts, School of Social Work and Family Studies, Forestry, Land and Food Science, Medicine, Science, Graduate Studies. Graduate Studies has had graduates from the School of Library, Archival, and Information Studies, Interdisciplinary Studies, and many other faculties.

We all know the reputation of students in engineering faculties, and incidents such as the time the UBC engineering students hung a car from the First Narrows Bridge in Vancouver. Their clash with First Nations students at UBC was not as clever. Some engineering students posted derogatory remarks toward First Nations students in their newsletter. They were immediately taken to task by the UBC Students' Union, which called a meeting of the engineering students and First Nations students. Many First Nations students spoke about how hurtful the remarks and portrayal of their people was to them, and about how difficult getting to university had been for them. The engineering students were polite and issued an apology for their actions. One of our Elders, Minnie Croft, spoke of how difficult a road it has been to get an education. She talked about her experiences at residential school. She urged them to help us, not to hinder us, as we were striving to better ourselves. The president of the engineering students bore the brunt of the incident and was required to meet with me to discuss ways to make amends and ways to further their understanding and better their appreciation of First Nations people.

After discussions with several people, I assigned him to do research on the Grease Trails—traditional Native trade routes from the Pacific coast to the BC interior—a subject I thought should interest an engineer, and to prepare a paper on it. I also required him to attend all of our First Nations Advisory Committee meetings for the year. He complied and became an ally. The Elders always provided us with good advice. They suggested that we hold a feast and invite the engineering students to attend. It was a potluck meal with traditional foods of salmon, wild meat, and *soopolallie* (in Chinook), soapberries used to make Indian ice cream, a treat among many First Nations in BC. They were invited, but not told what was planned. I'm sure it was with trepidation that they attended. The Elders, Chief Simon Baker, Minnie Croft, and Vince Stogan, spoke to the students about our ways, and while we were deeply hurt by their actions, it was time for forgiveness, which we were showing by giving them a feast. Many were deeply touched and gave their own heartfelt apologies. It was a memorable event. I'm not aware of any further negative incidents perpetrated by engineers on First Nations students, and First Nations students have graduated from engineering since then. Growth can come out of even sad situations if handled properly. Our Elders provided us with insight and wisdom to allow this to happen.

It wasn't all smooth sailing; it took a vision and a strong will to make changes in the university. The First Nations Advisory Committee stood strongly for change. We had an incident, for example, about tenure. I had been trying to get one of our faculty members on the tenure track and I was told that she did not have a PhD. I said that I had tenure and did not have a PhD. I was told that I had a lot of experience and that my case was different. I argued that if the person was working on a doctorate, he/she should be eligible. In fact, the university should be helping its Aboriginal faculty to attain their doctorates with paid time off at intervals to complete a doctorate in a shorter time. The advisory committee addressed this issue; finally, agreement was reached, and the matter would be reconsidered. The end result was good; the time-off suggestion was followed, and tenure track became an option. I'm not sure how long this practice was in place. Today, the number of Aboriginal tenured professors at UBC (with their doctorates) has grown significantly.

The mandate of the First Nations House of Learning is to make the university's vast resources more accessible to BC's First People and to improve the university's ability to meet the needs of First Nations. It is dedicated to quality preparation in all fields of post-secondary education, determined by its relevance to the philosophy and values of First Nations. The use of the term "First Nations" included Indians, Métis, and Inuit. The First Nations House of Learning objectives were as follows:

– To greatly increase the enrolments of First Nations
people in a wide range of study areas by actively
recruiting and providing support services.

– To expand the range and depth of program and
course offerings related to the need identified by First
Nations people and their communities in BC.

– To identify and promote research that would expand the
frontiers of knowledge for the benefit of First Nations of BC
(for example, legal studies of land claims and self-government,
resource management, delivery of social services).

– To increase the First Nations leadership on-campus.

– To establish a physical facility (longhouse) on campus to enhance
the recruitment and support services for First Nations students.

– A more long-range plan includes the possibility
of founding an international component for the
advancement of indigenous people around the world.[1]

In keeping with the objectives, in the course of the six years, we set the momentum in increasing the number of First Nations students at UBC and advancing the participation of First Nations students in areas beyond edu-

1. First Nations House of Learning Brochure, UBC, 1998.

cation and law. Our slogan became "1000 students by the year 2000." We worked with various faculties and departments interested in getting First Nations students into their respective fields. Education broadened out to specialized fields such as special education, social and educational studies, and curriculum instruction. We expanded to the graduate level. Our graduate students moved the research agenda through writing major papers, theses, and dissertations on topics related to Aboriginal issues. The Mokakit Indian Education Research Association was the research arm of our program. The increasing First Nations leadership was evident. In 1993, we opened the doors to the magnificent 25,000-square-metre longhouse situated prominently on the campus. The study tour I made to Hawaii, Australia, and New Zealand during my sabbatical leave in 1987 opened the doors to an international component of exchange in Indigenous interests.

My work at UBC kept me very busy, but I was always eager to pursue new ideas. In fact, it became a joke around the House of Learning when I would say, "I have an idea." The response would be—"Oh, oh, what are you thinking of now?" During these years at UBC, I was involved in several groundbreaking projects that made an impact in Aboriginal education, though they were not directly part of my job.

In 1984, I set about to establish what became the Mokakit Indian Education Research Association. For some time I had been thinking about the possibility of getting Aboriginal people with graduate degrees (master's and PhDs) together to discuss how we might impact research. These people had written theses and dissertations, so they had experience in research. I knew that very little research was being done by our people and that non-Natives were continuing to study us. At a conference in Ottawa, I met Roberta Miskokomon, an educator about my age with a master's degree. I expressed my concern to her and asked what she thought of inviting Native people with graduate degrees from across the country to Vancouver to talk about research. We decided that she would scout out such people in the eastern provinces and I would do the same in the western provinces. I set up a meeting at UBC to explore the possibilities and to see who might appear at this first meeting. Nine people showed up—Roberta Miskokomon and Dr. Roland Chrisjohn came from Ontario; Flora Zaharia and John Burelle from Manitoba; Marie

Smallface Marule, Joyce Goodstricker, and Camelia Dumont from Alberta; and Jo-ann Archibald and me from BC. I shared my thoughts with them concerning research. There was general agreement that there was a need for us to do something about this obvious void. We needed to know what research was out there, who was doing it, and, most importantly, what needed to be done by us to answer significant questions that concerned our people. We wasted no time getting organized. We even found a name for our group, *Mokakit,* which in the Blackfoot language means "in search of wisdom." I took on the task of registering us as a charitable organization so that we could apply for funding. We were all to keep trying to identify Native people with graduate degrees. I received some in-kind support from UBC, such as a meeting place and lunch. I referred to Mokakit as our research arm in Native education. At the time, there were very few people with graduate degrees, but our by-laws required members to be Native and have a graduate degree or equivalent.

We never got to be a big organization and at our highest had about thirty members, which in part was an indication of how few Indian people had graduate degrees at the time. We held our meetings in different parts of the country, including Calgary, Winnipeg, and Ottawa. We organized conferences and emphasized that only research papers would be accepted. Roland, who was an expert on computers, held pre-conference workshops to teach those who registered how to use computers in their research. In 1984–85, computers were still a rare commodity. We became well-known across the country and even in the United States, where strangely enough they did not have such an organization, though there were far more Native academics there than in Canada. Several U.S. Native academics gave papers at our conferences. We published the research papers and produced two volumes of research. Through this association, I got to meet great scholars like Dr. Carl Urion, a professor of education at the University of Alberta. Carl is about the best thinker I have come across in the Native world. We would become colleagues and good friends.

Since I was the founder and president of Mokakit, we were based at UBC. To get a handle on research related to Native issues at UBC, I organized a seminar and publicized it across the campus. Carl was invited to be the guest speaker to emphasize the importance of research in finding solutions to our people's issues and to discuss why Native people were suspicious about research. Over the years, non-Native academics, many of whom were anthropologists, had done research on Native people and published their work without the subjects of their research being properly consulted. Even Native researchers were suspect as a result. Research was a dirty word, and we would have to regain the confidence of our people. Some studies even measured the heads of Native people and concluded that we were not as intelligent as white people. Many other myths have been perpetuated by this kind of careless research. Our seminar was well attended by professors and graduate students, and we began to keep a record of what was being done at UBC, besides trying to find out what has been done elsewhere. It was important to have this information. I felt if we knew what was done across Canada we could see where the gaps were as we tried to make research a useful tool for us. I think we did get a measure of success by having this seminar. Researchers, especially non-Native graduate students, were now talking to us about their proposed research with Native subjects. Some I discouraged outright if I felt that what they proposed would not be helpful.

We accomplished a few important steps through Mokakit. We definitely put research on the Native agenda. Our goals included fostering higher education among Native Indians; promoting and enhancing individual and group research; reviewing and highlighting current research; conducting workshops and research seminars on research methodology; and holding research conferences and publishing a journal.

Our national conferences were open and well attended by Native and non-Native people alike. Many non-Native academics found a forum for their work. We would put out a call for papers and accepted only a certain number that could be accommodated at a three-day conference. Presenters were given a half-hour to highlight their topics and a further hour was provided for discussion.

I stepped down as president of Mokakit in 1987 when I took on further responsibilities at the university. My last conference as president was held in Yellowknife. Joe Handley, then head of education for the territorial government, was the main sponsor for this conference—and one of our members. We did not receive any operating dollars for Mokakit and managed to operate with membership fees. At one point, I advanced the organization $5,000 from my own pocket, which was repaid to me. For attendance at meetings, Mokakit members were responsible for their expenses. Most had good jobs and had their expenses covered. At the beginning of each meeting, those present had an opportunity to share information about their work. This usually led to a discussion of general education issues we faced. Mokakit served a meaningful function as a forum for Native education leaders to share with one another, be a support to one another, and to keep abreast of the goings-on in education throughout the country. At the last conference in my official capacity, they gave me a plaque recognizing my work as the founding president and I was made president emeritus of Mokakit. Jo-ann Archibald was elected to succeed me. During her tenure as president, funding was secured to work on several projects that included "First Nations Freedom: A Curriculum of Choice (alcohol, drug and substance abuse prevention), kindergarten to grade eight" and "Informing Myself and Informing Others: HIV/AIDS Curriculum for Aboriginal Youth, grades seven to twelve."

John and Flora were involved in full-time research for Mokakit. Jo-ann held the post for several years and was succeeded by Ethel Gardner. It was good to keep Mokakit at UBC, but the presidency went to Alberta when Ethel resigned to go to Harvard. Mokakit eventually became inactive. I suggested that we disband the organization properly, but the Alberta group felt that they could make it active again. Unfortunately, that never happened. I have heard very positive comments about Mokakit over the years, and its demise was unfortunate.

In 1986, I became involved with the *Canadian Journal of Native Education* while I was working with the Ts'kel graduate program. One day, I was approached by Dr. Robert Carney, a professor in the foundations department at the University of Alberta, responsible for creating the journal some years previously. He had the idea that rather than the University of Alberta putting out all three issues, it should be shared by UBC and the University of Saskatchewan. I went to Edmonton to meet Dr. Carney and his colleagues and I agreed to edit one of the three issues. Cecil King, also a first-wave academic, an Ojibway originally from Wikwemikong, Ontario, was in charge of Indian education at the University of Saskatchewan. He also agreed to be in charge of one of the issues. I had a lot of help from Val Friesen, the NITEP acting director, in the initial stages of this undertaking. The next year, Cecil did not do an issue. Later, only two issues of the journal were published each year. I continued to edit one issue per year right up until the time I retired from UBC in 1993. I encouraged our master's students to submit their major papers to the journal for publication. We didn't have an editorial board as such, and, basically, I decided, along with whomever was assisting me at the time, which articles to publish. For many years, Sheena Selkirk volunteered her services to the journal. Without her dedication to the project, I could not have continued, as I had extremely heavy responsibilities. The *Canadian Journal of Native Education* is still published by the University of Alberta and First Nations House of Learning (UBC). Jo-ann took over after I left; she is still involved as editor of the UBC issue. The format has a much classier look and is now a refereed journal. I'm pleased to have had a number of articles published in the journal throughout the years, as it continues to be a popular forum for Aboriginal research and one of the most referenced Native journals in existence.

Another exciting development for me was organizing the first World Conference of Indigenous People in Education in 1987. It was during a Multicultural and Native Indian Education Conference in Vancouver in 1985 that I presented the idea that we should have our own conference on Native Indian education. I held a poster session, inviting people interested in exploring this idea to join me. Several did, and we soon were talking about a world conference. We formed an International Indigenous Peoples' Education Association, with membership of both Indigenous and non-Indigenous people who shared common interests and goals. This included believing that educational success of Indigenous people lies in applying traditional values and beliefs to contemporary educational practices. We planned to hold a world conference in June 1987 based on the theme "Tradition, Change and Survival" and the sub-theme "the answers are within us."

In 1986, prior to the conference, we held a roundtable in Vancouver to discuss the general shape of our conference program. A panel of twelve educators and Elders from seven countries discussed issues in traditional education for a contemporary world before an audience of 100 delegates. We also invited presentations from Indigenous schools considered to have made progress in controlling their own schools.

The first World Conference of Indigenous People in Education was held June 8 to 13, 1987, in Vancouver. The opening day was held at Xwmelch'sten, the site of the Squamish Nation, where we gathered together in the Longhouse for the opening ceremonies. Fifteen hundred people from seventeen countries were represented and sat in groups. It was an amazing sight. Following the protocol of the Squamish Nation, speeches were made and gifts exchanged by the host and the visitors. The day continued with demonstrations of traditional forms of education. There was a large stage for singing and dancing, a tent for the performing arts, an Elders' tent for storytelling, an area showing various ways of cooking salmon, a games area, and so on. Having our first day at Xwmelch'sten set the tone for the conference that would take a more formal format when it moved on to the UBC campus.

Keynote speeches, paper presentations, workshops all addressed some aspect of the importance of having culture as the basis of learning, holistic learning—cognitive, spiritual, physical and emotional growth, and ownership of education. By all measures it was a successful conference, one of many to follow.

Since then, the conferences, now known as WIPCE, World Indigenous Peoples' Conference on Education, take place triennially, with meetings having been held in New Zealand, Australia, Hawaii, mainland USA, and Peru. It was back in Canada in 2002, at Stoney Park, Nakoda Nation, in Morley, Alberta. The size of the conference has grown to the thousands, and many more countries are represented. What started as an idea in 1985 has stood the test of time, and we have all benefitted from the gathering of nations.

STUDY TOURS TO AOTEAROA (NEW ZEALAND)

In 1987, with the world conference planning well underway, I took a three-month sabbatical leave. I planned to research Indigenous education among the Hawaiians, the Australian Aborigines, and the Maori people of Aotearoa (the land of the long white cloud). My findings were interesting in that it appeared to me that we Canadians were progressing in line with the Hawaiians, were twenty years ahead of Australia, and twenty years behind New Zealand.

I had another reason to travel to other countries at this time and it was to spread the word about our upcoming world conference on the education of Indigenous people. It proved worthwhile, as we had a large contingent from Aoteroa and a significant presence from Australia and Hawaii.

"Discovering" the Maori people was very significant, not only for what I would learn from them, but for the lasting relationship that developed between them and our people.

I was very impressed with all the advances they were making, especially in the areas of education, employment, and, most of all, their language renewal program. The loss of our Native languages in Canada was and continues to be a serious problem. I knew that we could benefit from learning about Te Kohanga Reo (Maori language nests), their early language renewal program. In short, Maori grandfathers and grandmothers, who were fluent in the language, were teaching the Maori language to children from babies to age five. They believed that babies internalize language early through exposure to the language. The Kohanga Reo programs were located on *maraes* (Maori meeting places) or in areas adjacent to common places where the children's parents were employed. The program leaders had decided not to worry about the parents of the children who had lost the language. The Kohanga Reo was language immersion and only Maori could be spoken. If parents came to help with lunch or for any other reason they were not to speak to the children unless it was in Maori. The children progressed very well; soon their parents became interested in learning the language and classes were offered to assist them. In the Kohanga Reo, they did not have the toys found in typical preschools. Instead, they had to make all their own toys. By working with children, instructing them on how to make the toys, the grandparents passed on language. The program operated in what they referred to as *whanau* (family) style. In other words, children spent the day doing typical things that children do when at home. They played, they sang, they painted, and they ate. "Talk, talk, talk" was the mantra of the leaders of the program. Singing is a great part of the Maori culture, and being a visitor to New Zealand on those many occasions, I felt that all Maori people were great singers.

I loved the revival of the language that I saw in Aotearoa. This is what prompted me to organize tours of people from Canada to witness what was happening in this country. Among those interested in language who signed up for these tours were teachers, parents, grandparents, Elders, and students. There was a great deal of interest across Canada and in the state of Alaska, so it was not difficult to get groups of thirty to forty eager participants together for each the eight tours we went on. Once again, I had the capable help of Sheena Selkirk to organize these tours. In all cases, participants were charged a fee to cover their travel and accommodation. It was each person's responsibility to pay his or her own way.

Not only did we learn about the process and the methods the Maori used to revive the language, but as visitors we were immersed in their culture, which, of course, goes hand in hand with language. Whenever we arrived at a marae, we had to follow the customs and protocol of the Maori people. The *whare nui*, the sleeping house, is the main house on the marae. The building is adorned with carved poles that tell the history of the tribal group to which it belonged. Pictures of their early ancestors and more recent Elders are hung on the walls or placed around the room. It is a place where meetings, weddings, and funerals are held. It contains no chairs or chesterfields, and everyone is expected to sit on the floor. The size of these buildings we visited varied and held anywhere from thirty to sixty or more people. This was a rare experience for the people I took there. Mattresses were placed around the periphery of the large room. Clean sheets and pillows were provided. Whoever stayed there was expected to bring a sleeping bag or blanket. Washrooms were typically in another building. Men and women had separate washrooms with showers, but slept side by side. One mattress was placed right next to the other. It was not easy to get comfortable in this communal living arrangement. Imagine fifty or sixty people all sleeping in the same room and you know there will be snoring—lots of snoring. I remember one of the men with us who seemed particularly uncomfortable with this setup. As time went on, he lost all his inhibitions and, on the last night, there he was in his pajamas walking around with his video camera.

Other buildings on the marae consist of the *whare kai*, the dining area, and sometimes a church. Most marae do not have permanent residents as they did in the old days. Today, it is the place where special events and meetings are held and where Maori customs are given ultimate expression.

Whenever newcomers enter a marae, there is a welcome ceremony called a *powhiri*, which serves to ward off evil spirits that may be present. The hosts gather to greet you. In our case, our entourage would approach the gate. A host member, usually an Elder woman, would join us to take us on to the marae. We would move about halfway up the courtyard. When the *karanga*, a spiritual welcome call of the host woman Elder, was heard, we moved closer toward the hosts. Speeches began, first by three or four of the hosts telling us of their ancestors and their history, all in the Maori language. Each speech was followed by a *waiata,* a song. Then the visitors spoke. Only men are allowed to give speeches on the marae. I was prepared for this and asked three men to speak at each marae. If our speakers knew their Native language, they used it; otherwise, it was in English. The speeches were followed by the challenge. Originally, this was to find out whether the visiting party came in peace or war. One of the more well-known challenges is the *haka*, which is performed before the New Zealand All Blacks rugby games.

Because we were visitors planning to stay for a day or more, the last speaker of our group placed an envelope down on the ground. It was our *koha,* the donation we gave for our stay at the marae. A woman from the host tribe performed the *karanga* to indicate thanks for the *koha*, and one of the men picked up the envelope. The visitors were then invited to meet the people by shaking hands and doing the *hongi,* the pressing of noses (the foreheads touch; it is a sharing of thoughts and emotions). This whole experience was very moving and meaningful to us as we witnessed how seriously the Maori carry out the traditional ways of their ancestors.

I believe that these excursions, usually of two-week duration, raised the awareness level of our people and motivated them to make a greater effort toward language renewal. As a result, there are a few centres in Canada modelled after the Kohanga Reo.

After retirement, I would accompany two more tours to Aotearoa to study the Maori language initiatives. By returning several times after my initial visit in 1987 (my last study venture was in 2003), I was able to see the progress of the language program as it extended from pre-school to the university. In fact, it is possible for a person today to graduate from university knowing only the Maori language. Of course, most Maori people are fluent in English but choose the Maori immersion route to preserve their language. The Maori people make up about 17 percent of the population of New Zealand. The revival of the language has changed the English language significantly, and many Maori words and phrases have become standard vocabulary for the *pakeha* (non-Maoris). Both use the greeting *Kia Ora,* meaning "hello" or "how are you?" Maori is an offical language in New Zealand.

FEASIBILITY STUDY ON AN ABORIGINAL LANGUAGES INSTITUTE

In 1984, at a First Ministers' conference, Prime Minister Trudeau, responding to pressure from Aboriginal leaders, directed the federal government to preserve and enhance the cultural and linguistic heritage of Canada's Aboriginal people. The result of the directive was that the Department of the Secretary of State commissioned a major review of the state of Aboriginal languages in Canada. Many reports were submitted by researchers. Most startling was the fact that of the fifty-three distinct Aboriginal languages still spoken in Canada, only three were predicted to survive (Cree, Ojibway, and Inuktitut). Following the review, the Assembly of First Nations, sponsored by the Secretary of State, formed a committee to identify an Aboriginal languages policy.

I was invited to attend a conference in January of 1988 where the proposed policy would be discussed and presented to the Secretary of State and Minister of Multiculturalism David Crombie. One of the prominent chiefs of an Ontario Indian organization, an astute politician, approached me and suggested we talk to the minister beforehand and suggest to him that an Aboriginal Languages Institute be created, comparable to the Heritage Language Institute that had recently been formed by his department. We spoke to the minister before the session began, and he liked the idea. That's when all hell broke loose! After the minister announced that an Aboriginal languages institute would be formed, there was an uproar from those who had worked on the policy. The Assembly of First Nations expected the minister to speak to the policy and rejected the idea of an institute because it had not previously been discussed with them. It was not the intention of the chief or me to usurp attention to the Aboriginal languages policy; rather we saw this as a mechanism through which language renewal work could be undertaken.

It was shortly after this, in March of 1988, that Minister Crombie approached me to do a two-month feasibility study to examine whether an Aboriginal languages institute should be established, and if so, to recommend the most suitable model for the founding of such an institute. A former deputy minister of Indian Affairs was hired to work with me on the research. I travelled across Canada meeting with key individuals and groups with a language interest to get their reaction to the formation of an Aboriginal languages institute. It was not difficult to ascertain from these meetings that there was no overwhelming support for an institute, mainly because it had the connotation of a building, or an establishment such as a university or college with a centrally controlled operation. The message from the people was that they wanted to control their own language initiatives, but they needed the money to do this.

I spoke to the people at the Donner Canadian Foundation to get their opinion about whether a foundation would work as a way to secure monies for local Aboriginal language initiatives. It appeared to be the best option to meet community needs. We recommended that an Aboriginal languages foundation be established by the Secretary of State to ensure the perpetuation, revitalization, growth, and protection of Aboriginal languages in Canada, and that the foundation be endowed with $100 million. We stated that the mandate, functions, and activities would be carried out by the foundation to promote local language initiatives. The report was accepted by the Secretary of State and given to the Assembly of First Nations for their reaction.

Work by the Assembly of First Nations on the Aboriginal languages policy had been ongoing, and when it was completed the AFN sponsored a national conference to seek reaction and subsequent approval from the chiefs of Canada. Prior to this conference, the consultant for the AFN had called me and asked if I minded if she presented the Aboriginal Languages Foundation report to the chiefs. I was delighted with this idea, as the Secretary of State was seeking the agreement of the AFN before establishing the foundation. Our report recommending an Aboriginal Languages Foundation was overwhelmingly accepted by the chiefs. However, there was a delay in the

AFN office in providing the approval of the chiefs to the Secretary of State. We faced a federal election, with the government in power going down. The initiative was lost. Later, Ethel Blondin, an Aboriginal woman who was a member of Parliament for the Northwest Territories, brought it forward as a private member's bill, but with no positive result.

In a huge study by the Royal Commission on Aboriginal Peoples in 1996, once again an Aboriginal languages foundation was recommended. It has not happened; instead, over the years, the federal government has spent hundreds of thousands of dollars engaging numerous task forces and other studies to determine the state of Aboriginal languages ad nauseam, with little or no money reaching the communities where it is needed. The problem gets worse with each passing year. Even though my language, Cree, was one of the three predicted to survive, I know that there are fewer and fewer speakers as the grandparents pass away. The idea of an Aboriginal languages foundation is still a viable option. After I retired from UBC, I did some work for the First Nations Confederacy of Cultural Education Centres (FNCCEC) to continue the battle to address this growing problem of the loss of our languages.

THE FIRST NATIONS LONGHOUSE

As director of Native Indian Education, I was informed that our hut was scheduled for demolition. They didn't say when but I knew we must prepare for that eventuality. That was when I first suggested that we should have our own building, a longhouse. It became one of the objectives of the First Nations House of Learning. A physical facility on campus would enhance access and support services for First Nations students. It was, of course, a dream. How could that ever happen? Still, dreams do come true, as this one did. For me, it was like having another full-time job, yet the creation of this dream stands out as a great achievement.

In January of 1989, I convened the first meeting of students, Elders, and our staff to discuss the concept of a longhouse on campus. There was much excitement over this possibility. In March I held a second meeting, this time to talk about what we would like to see included in the longhouse. The brainstorming session revealed that we should have a student lounge, a computer room, a great hall, a kitchen, a library, a daycare centre, a carving room, and a jewellery shop, along with offices. I met with President Strangway and Vice-President Birch to present our dream of building a longhouse on campus that would serve as our students' home away from home. They were interested in the prospect, but somewhat skeptical of such a giant undertaking. In their usual response to new ideas, they said they would consider it.

On March 17, 1989—this date is indelibly fixed in my mind—I received a call from President Strangway to inform me that Mr. Jack Bell, a philanthropist, who made his money on peat moss, cranberries, and golf courses had donated $1 million to First Nations at UBC. Dr. Strangway said, "This may be the beginning of your longhouse." He loved to tell the story of the day he received the donation. He had been invited to have lunch with Jack Bell in a downtown restaurant. When they had finished, Jack Bell turned to Dr. Strangway and said, "If you get the bill, I will give you this," as he handed him a cheque, which he said was for First Nations at UBC. What an exciting St. Patrick's Day that was for me! Mr. Bell had not specified what should be done with the gift, and Dr. Strangway left it to me to decide what we should do with the money.

I immediately set out to meet with the First Nations Indian Education Advisory Committee and the First Nations House of Learning Advisory Committee and held a special meeting with our students, faculty, and staff. My question was "Should we put this donation toward the building of our longhouse?" The other option was to put it toward scholarships and bursaries.

It was fortuitous that the university had just launched the UBC World of Opportunity Campaign. In this campaign, the province had agreed to match dollars for capital projects. With the gift from Mr. Bell, we became part of the campaign and our million dollars quickly became two million. I don't know if Jack Bell realized the significance of his gift at this very crucial time. He was pivotal to the realization of our dream. The final cost would be over $5 million.

My first step was to strike a building committee, which I chaired. First Nations Elders, students, faculty, and staff comprised the committee to oversee the project. I wanted this project to be driven by us. We included a coordinator from the university's development office because more money had to be raised if we were to succeed.

We, the First Nations students, Elders, faculty, and staff, actually spearheaded the project, a rare opportunity not often enjoyed by First Nations people on a university campus.

We determined what would be contained in the longhouse, where it would be located, who our architect would be. We decided what ceremonies we would have to mark significant milestones as we progressed. Following the West Coast First Nations tradition, we held ceremonies to mark the site dedication, ground blessing, sod turning, and house post and roof-beam raising. We had a longhouse cleansing ceremony prior to our official move, followed by the grand opening. I learned a lot during this time about West Coast First Nations in general and about the Musqueam in particular, since UBC lies on the traditional territory of the Musqueam Nation. I learned from our committees and other interested parties how to honour the cultures and protocols of the original inhabitants of the land. All of our meetings and gatherings began and ended with a prayer to the Creator. As a prairie Cree woman, I had to be a good listener and a person of action to steer this project along.

With the effort of many people, the president's office, the development office, the planning office, the Museum of Anthropology staff, the provincial government, community people, our own students and staff, and our building committee members, we moved into our magnificent 2,043-square-metre Coast Salish–style longhouse on March 15, 1993, just four years after we received our gift from Jack Bell. Ours was the second capital project to be completed on campus through the World of Opportunity Campaign.

On May 25, 1993, we had our grand opening celebration, which lasted for four days. On May 26, the Native Indian Teacher Education Program hosted events, on the 27th, the BC First Nations Chapter of the American Indian Science and Engineering Society (AISES) hosted a health sciences symposium, and on the final day the International Conference on Higher Education was hosted by the University of Alaska as a prelude to their Canadian Indian Teacher Education (CITEP) Conference, which carried on immediately from these events. A number of us went on to Anchorage, Alaska, to take part in the conference.

Interested Indigenous people from other countries came to see our long-house and to join in our festivities, including the president of Yakutia in Russia, and prominent Indigenous educators from New Zealand, Australia, the United States, and across Canada. At this point, most of the UBC First Nations graduates were in the Faculty of Education. The university arranged the graduation calendar for Education to coincide with the grand opening. They were the special honourees of the day. Several hundred people gathered at the entrance to the longhouse, where the large patio served as the stage for the opening ceremonies. I gave the opening address:

> Grandmothers, Grandfathers, Sisters and Brothers, Grandchildren
> from the Four Directions, welcome to the First Nations
> Longhouse at the University of British Columbia. We are
> honoured that you have journeyed here from far and near to
> witness this special occasion and to join us in our celebration. We
> thank the Great Spirit for bringing you safely to us and for giving
> us this beautiful day that we may unite in love and harmony.

> The Longhouse is a symbol of love, harmony and a strong
> belief in a spiritual power that can make all things possible.
> From the fall of 1989, our students, our Elders, faculty and
> staff representing many different Nations worked together
> through long hours of workshops to provide direction
> and guidance to the building of this Longhouse.

> – We wanted the Longhouse to be "our home
> away from home" where children and Elders had a
> prominent place in the daily lives of the students.

> – We wanted the Longhouse to be a place where our
> heritage was respected and our cultures could thrive.

> – We wanted the Longhouse to be a place where we could
> share our knowledge and cultures with one another.

> – We wanted the Longhouse to be a place where we
> could share our knowledge and cultures with the general
> university and community and the larger society.

Together we gather to celebrate a dream come true, a
vision to benefit future generations of children yet unborn.
We are, indeed, fortunate to see on a university campus,
as Sharilyn Calliou remarked, "a dramatic reminder
of the presence of the original inhabitants of this land
and their future as leaders in a changing world."

On behalf of our students, Elders, faculty and staff, I lift my hands
in praise and thanksgiving to every person who was involved in
any way in this magnificent Longhouse that stands here today.

Thank you to each and every one of you who have come to
witness and celebrate with us. In keeping with tradition,
we invite you to enjoy the four-day gathering.

To my surprise and delight the Maori contingent sang a *waita* at the end
of my address, as is their custom. They join together in song after speeches are
given. This filled my heart, as I had come to know and love the Maori people.

In addition to my welcoming address, there were other speeches and, according to BC First Nations tradition, witnesses were named. The witnesses
were to remember this day, and to let others know what they witnessed, and
to spread the good word. Each was given time to speak. My cousin, Patricia
Beyer, from Manitoba, Alphie Waugh, a First Nations graduate in architecture
who worked with the architects on the longhouse, and Margaret Valadian, an
educator from Australia, were the witnesses.

Several presentations were made. President Strangway was given the Haida
name, Kil Sli, by Elder Minnie Croft and her niece Terri-Lynn, while draping
on him a beautiful button blanket saying, "I have the pleasant and enjoyable
duty of presenting our Eagle ceremonial blanket and a new Haida name to the
President of the University of British Columbia.... Kil Sli is a name bestowed
on a person we feel deserves a high honour.... You are a great man! Without
your commitment to our Native people, we would not be standing by this very
beautiful longhouse today."

Cree Elders Ahab and Bette Spence and I, with witnesses Elder Margaret
White and Kathy Louis, presented a large mandala featuring an eagle, a sym-
bol of greatness in many Aboriginal societies, to Dan Birch, and bestowed

upon him a Cree name. I acknowledged him by saying, "In recognition of the compassion, understanding and commitment... to the advancement of Aboriginal education we bestow upon you the Cree name Mitêhe, which in the language of the Cree people means 'heart' with the spiritual connotation of 'life'. With the support you have given us, progress has been made toward making the University of British Columbia a more relevant and friendly place for Aboriginal students." I appreciated the very special relationship I had with Dan and his wife Arlene for their loyalty and friendship. Later, they would endow the Verna J. Kirkness (Ni-Jing-Jada) Scholarship on my behalf shortly after I left UBC. Each year, worthy students in graduate studies are awarded a scholarship from this endowment.

I was deeply touched when the students, Oscar, Beverly, Phillip, and Ellen presented me with a beautiful button blanket that had been made by the students. Oscar's words were: "On behalf of the students past, present and future, we'd like to thank you, Verna. The crest that you see on the button blanket symbolizes the wealth of the Native people. In the copper, we have included the First Nations House of Learning logo. Certainly, Verna, your contribution to First Nations, especially here in BC, will not be forgotten."

I felt totally blessed that day to see our dream become a reality and the happiness felt by so many. The Elders that had been involved throughout the project marvelled that they were able to see a project dear to their hearts actually happen in their lifetime. Twenty years later, the aroma of the cedar still penetrates the building. Our hopes and dreams for its purpose have manifested itself many times over.

Each year, the First Nations graduates gather with their parents, spouses, children, and friends in Sty-Wet-Tan, the name of the Great Hall. The name was given to Mr. Jack Bell to honour him for his gift. Rather than call it the Jack Bell Hall, the Musqueam people gave him the name meaning "Spirit of the West Wind." Other major donors were honoured in the same way. Mr. William Bellman, who also gave $1 million, was given the name X̱wi7x̱wa. Mr. Bellman was a CBC radio host and founder of Vancouver radio station CHQM. The library was named after him. The third big donor was James Wallace, a real estate developer and owner of the Wallace Neon Company. He gave $500,000 and was given the name Wii Ax (a tall, hardy mountain fern) by the Gitksan Nation. This became the name of the administrative unit of the longhouse.

On the day of graduation, as a special honour the graduates enter through the Eastern door that is used only for special occasions. They are introduced as they enter, while relatives and friends look on with pride. The First Nations students appreciate and enjoy having this wonderful space as their own.

I retired from UBC on June 30, 1993, just three months after we moved into the Longhouse. It was a difficult decision for me to come to, as I was only fifty-seven years old. My three-year contract had led to twelve years. It was my feeling that it was time to leave because other BC First Nations faculty could take over the responsibilities I held. By this time, I was satisfied that I had met the objective set out when I was first hired as a supervisor of NITEP to increase the number of British Columbia First Nations faculty and staff. All but one faculty member, a valued person in NITEP (not counting the professors) were First Nations. All the House of Learning staff were First Nations, as were the lecturers for the Native Studies courses. Most of the members of the advisory committees were First Nations. We had a definite presence on campus.

By this time, my career had spanned nearly forty years. I had taken only two years off during that time to study (most of my education was completed while working, by correspondence or summer school). I think the bottom line was that I was very tired and feared that I would burn out. I felt that I should make a complete break to allow other leadership to emerge. I gave no thought about what I would do next or for that matter what kind of a pension I would have to live on. I had no alternative plan.

In preparation for my departure, I went about restructuring the job responsibilities I had for consideration by my superiors. The head of NITEP was still a supervisor. I recommended that the head be designated a director in full charge of the program. As director of Native Indian Education, I oversaw NITEP and the Ts'kel graduate programs. I recommended that the head of Ts'kel also be designated a director. This would be a more realistic load than to have one person in charge of these programs and the House of Learning as well. The recommendations were accepted.

Before I left UBC, I made it clear that I didn't want a farewell party of any kind. I wanted to just walk out the doors to my condominium for a good long rest. I was content with what I had been a part of during those years. I loved the job and the wonderful people of BC who accepted me, the little prairie Cree woman, to have a share in their lives.

In November of 1993, a party was held in Sty-Wet-Tan in my honour. When Jo-ann Archibald, who was hired as my successor, called me to tell me they were planning a party for me, I reminded her that I had said I did not want a party. She said, "Well, you are not the boss now." It was a lovely gesture on their part to do this. I invited my niece from Manitoba, who came with her four-month-old son, Zach. It wasn't often that any members of my family were able to be present at these special functions because of the distance. I also invited my old friend and roommate Beverly from my normal school days and her husband, who now lived in Victoria. Many people from the university, including the president and vice-president (academic) were present. The university's gift to me was a lap-top computer. I guess they realized I would no longer have a secretary. (It took me a few months before I took it out of the box. In the end, it was a godsend.) Community members and students were present. Before this grand group of people, Minnie Croft, one of our Elders, bestowed on me the Haida name Ni-Jing-Jada, which means longhouse lady. I am deeply honoured to hold this Haida name. Oh, what a grand night it was with all the people I worked with in some way present, the generous accolades, the lovely gifts, and a huge cake that read "Thank You Verna."

As I reflect on my time at UBC, I believe that my arrival there was timely. I was ready for a new challenge in advancing Aboriginal education and UBC was interested in making its vast resources more accessible to Aboriginal people. I had gone the gamut from teaching, to counselling, to supervising teachers, to developing curriculum suitable for Aboriginal children and youth, to working in policy development with provincial and national Aboriginal organizations. With this background, the challenge of working at the university level proved to be a good match.

CHAPTER SIX

Retirement

I HAD MADE ONE OF THE BIGGEST decisions of my life—to retire. Huge as this move was, I had given little thought to what I would do in retirement or what pension I would get.

All I knew was that it was time for me to leave UBC, as a new era was beginning with a new home in the Longhouse for students and staff. My life had always unfolded in interesting ways. In my heart, I left my future to divine guidance.

After many years of getting up in the morning with a definite schedule in mind, it is a shock to the system not to have to do it anymore. It was like having a blank slate in front of me. If any thoughts ever went through my mind about retirement, it was that I would do all the things I never had time to do while on the job. What on earth were those things?

I was definite about a few matters, one being that I was not interested in another full-time job. I was invited to submit an application for interesting positions which, if offered earlier in my life, would have been tempting. Doing any kind of work at UBC, be it by contract or voluntarily, was also not in my plan, simply because I did not want any appearance of interfering with the new leadership at the First Nations House of Learning. I had complete faith in their ability to carry on.

There was one very important task that I had to attend to, which was to complete the writing of Chief Simon Baker's book. In 1994, a year after my retirement, *Khot-La-Cha: The Autobiography of Chief Simon Baker* was published by Douglas and McIntyre. With his photo on the cover, showing Simon dressed in his Squamish regalia, it was a book that he was truly proud to share with everyone.

Because of Simon's involvement as an Elder in the building of the First Nations Longhouse at UBC, it was fitting that the book launch was held there in Sty-Wet-Tan, the Great Hall. Many people attended the launch. In the Coast Salish tradition, Simon was honoured in a ceremony, and with great pride he autographed books. I treasure my copy of the book inscribed by Simon. He wrote, "You have made my day. Our friendship will live for all times. Good work, Verna. My sincere love to you and others. Chief Khot La Cha, Kind Heart." Over 5,000 copies of the book were sold, and with the royalties I endowed the Khot La Cha Award at the University of British Columbia. Each year, the award is offered to a First Nations student who is engaged in research involving Elders.

I have never considered myself an author, though I have written several books and have had many articles published in books and journals in Canada and other countries. After Simon's book was completed, I did go on to further writing. One of my gravest concerns over the years has been the loss of our Aboriginal languages. It is the reason I initiated the Manitoba Native Bilingual Program for nursery to grade three back in the early seventies, did the study for the Secretary of State that recommended an Aboriginal Languages Foundation, wrote many articles on the topic, several of which were published in the *First Nations Perspective* newspaper, and organized tours to Aotearoa to study their early childhood language renewal program, the Kōhanga Reo.

I welcomed the opportunity to continue to work in the area of languages when I was approached by the First Nations Confederacy of Cultural Education Centres (FNCCEC) to research, compile, and analyze information, policies, and legislation leading to the development of protective legislation for Aboriginal languages in Canada. Being once again immersed in the topic of our languages, I decided to write a book that would include a collection of my works in Aboriginal languages over the years. I hoped that this collection would in some small way provide an historical context of the state of our languages and our efforts to preserve, protect, practise, and promote them over the years. This book, entitled *Aboriginal Languages: A Collection of Talks and Papers*, was self-published in 1998.

In 1999, I compiled and edited a book entitled *O Great Creator: A Collection of Works*, by Ruth Spence. Ruth and her late husband, Dr. Ahab Spence, have been my mentors for many years. During one of my summer visits home to Manitoba, I stopped by to see them in Regina, Saskatchewan. I brought up the subject of Ahab's memoirs, trying to encourage him to get these written. Instead, he told me his wife had a whole scribbler full of hand-written prayers she had composed over the years that should be published. She showed these to me, and I suggested that I type them and put them in verse form. It was a self-published book which still sits prominently in the collection of family, community members, friends, and students alike.

The building of the Longhouse at UBC was such a unique experience. I thought it would be a good idea to document the process involved in its construction. I wanted people to know that the concept of the Longhouse, a "home away from home" for Aboriginal students at UBC, was driven right from the beginning by the Aboriginal students, Elders, faculty, and staff at UBC. I think it is rare among universities to extend such trust and confidence in Aboriginal people. It was early after my retirement that the idea for this book occurred to me. Over the years, I worked on it from time to time. Finally, when I got really serious about it, the Longhouse had been in existence for several years. I invited Jo-ann Archibald to co-author the book with me by writing the latter section, as she had succeeded me and had worked in the Longhouse ever since. *The First Nations Longhouse: Our Home Away from Home* was published by UBC Press in 2001.

During the course of my career, my works appeared in books and journals nationally and internationally. I have given many speeches, papers, and addresses in my lifetime, many of which I kept in my filing cabinet. When I retired from UBC, I left a binder of this collection in the X̱wi7x̱wa Library at the First Nations Longhouse. The collection has been digitized and it is now available online (see Appendix 3).

Ever since I retired, I seem to have a very full life, and certainly always have something interesting to work on. I have not left behind my interest in Indigenous education and continue to participate in a number of ways. Besides writing, I have guest lectured at universities and conferences, engaged in contract work, served on several boards and committees, initiated a new program, travelled, and even tried living common-law, all of which have been interesting though not always successful.

I had two very different experiences as a visiting professor. In 2002, I was invited to Brandon University as a Stanley Knowles Visiting Professor for a three-month period during the spring term. Since Brandon University had the largest enrolment of Aboriginal students of any university in Manitoba, I was interested in being a part of it. Most of the students were in education, as the Program for the Education of Native Teachers (PENT) and the Brandon University Northern Teacher Education Program (BUNTEP), a community-based program, had been offered there since the 1970s.

I don't know what had prompted my invitation because, to my disappointment, I found no particular arrangements had been made for my stay, no apparent expectations provided, and not a great deal of interest taken in my visit. It was several days before I was officially introduced to the faculty at a reception. A few of the professors did invite me to speak to their classes, I spoke to the PENT students at their orientation, visited a nearby BUNTEP Centre, and gave three of the four public lectures I planned to give. I did not feel that I was in any way being fully utilized.

I was pleased when finally, one day, I was asked to participate in a specific task, the rejuvenation of the Master of Education Program – Aboriginal Specialization. This was a familiar area for me, as I had been involved in such work at UBC. I learned that 30 percent of the undergraduate enrolment at the university was Aboriginal, therefore the potential for students in graduate studies was enormous. I also learned that at least 100 Aboriginal students had been enrolled in a Master of Education program within the last ten years, most of whom only completed partial requirements. I hoped that a number of these students could be enticed to return to complete their master's. Before the work could even begin, I learned through the grapevine that a decision had been made to eliminate the Aboriginal specialization from the Master of Education offerings. I received no official notification of this decision. Although it was out of character for me to leave before my term was up, with no apparent expectations of me, I decided it was time to leave.

My second experience in being a guest lecturer was at Memorial University in St. John's, Newfoundland, in 2005. I was invited as a guest lecturer for the Henrietta Maxwell Distinguished Lecture Series. I spent a busy week there speaking in a number of classes and giving one major address that was open to the public. This lecture was very well attended, which indicated a strong interest in Aboriginal education even though there was a low number of Aboriginal students on campus. I had occasion to give a video conference lecture to a class in Labrador, where the university offers programs. It was an amazing experience, as it was the first time I had presented in this way. Oh, the marvels of technology! Overall, I had a great time at Memorial University. The faculty members were wonderful hosts and kept me busy with a full itinerary, including a sightseeing tour, and dinners at restaurants and the homes of the professors.

This visit to St. John's had another special aspect to it for me. It was in February and the Scott Tournament of Hearts curling final was being held in that city. Our Manitoba team, skipped by Jennifer Jones, was in the final against Ontario. I decided it would be a wonderful opportunity to see the game. I contacted the hosts and requested that I arrive a day earlier to take in the game. A former acquaintance of mine who was a professor at Memorial University purchased tickets and accompanied me to the game. We had excellent seats near the front. The game was not going in Manitoba's favour, and in the last end our team was trailing by two points. With a magnificent shot by Jennifer, a shot still shown on curling highlights, Manitoba scored three points to win the championship. I did not realize that I had been cheering loudly until a person sitting behind us congratulated me on our team's win. I'm sure she thought I must be connected to the curling family in some way because of my enthusiasm for the game.

I have had the privilege of working on two major contracts, one of which was with the First Nations Confederacy of Cultural Education Centres that I spoke of earlier and the other with the Manitoba Government. Shortly after I left Brandon in 2002, I was approached by Manitoba's deputy minister of Advanced Education and Training to lead a consultation team into northern communities to discuss post-secondary education and to solicit views on how this could be delivered. The Aboriginal people, who are in the majority in northern Manitoba, had for many years been making formal requests for a university college in the north. In a message from the minister, Hon. Diane McGifford, she referred to the Manitoba Keewatinowi Okimakanak's September 2000 paper, "The University College of the North: A Vision for Our Future." She acknowledged that the debate over post-secondary education services in northern Manitoba had been going on for almost fifteen years and she was determined to take the subject from debate to action.

The consultation team consisted of two government employees, one of whom was a technician to videotape the sessions. I requested that another member be added from the Department of Education, Training, and Youth, an Aboriginal woman with extensive knowledge of Aboriginal education and a Cree speaker. Her language skills were essential, as Cree was spoken by many of the older people in the communities. The government had prepared a format for our consultation sessions, complete with visuals. We began our travels in September to conduct our meetings. In all, we visited twelve communities in the north, nine of which were First Nations communities, along with The Pas, Thompson, and Flin Flon. Accommodation was made to fly representatives from outlying communities to the major centres, as it was impossible for us to visit every community. We held meetings at the universities of Brandon, Manitoba, and Winnipeg, as well as with Manitoba Hydro, and we received written submissions from groups and individuals. Overall, there was strong support for the establishment of a university college in the north with programming that would reflect its population.

November and December were certainly not the best times to be travelling in northern Manitoba, as we encountered both rain and snow. Travel in the north is usually by small planes. I suggested that we travel the same way the people from the communities do, by scheduled flights rather than chartering planes. I felt this would give the team a realistic experience in northern travel. On our visit to St. Theresa Point, the pilot made two attempts to land, but due to poor weather and limited visibility, each time he aborted the landing. He then informed us that we would have to fly to Thompson to fuel up. Once there, it felt great to have our feet on solid ground. After a quick cup of coffee in the airport, we were off again flying through dense clouds to our destination. We finally landed safely, but were a bit shaken. It had been snowing, and by some miscommunication the party to meet us had heard that we would not be coming. Fortunately, I knew one of the passengers on the flight who had someone meet him and he offered the two of us women a ride. We left the two men behind with their luggage and promised that we would send someone for them. Shortly after we arrived at the hotel, they appeared, riding on the back of a truck. They were not familiar with northern travel to remote locations and had quite the tales to tell about this adventure.

At our consultation meetings, I presented several key issues for discussion, including the principles and mission of a northern institution, the program mix, regional coverage, and how to reflect the Aboriginal reality and cultural diversity of the north. Some participants presented briefs individually from their constituencies, whether it was a family, institution, town, or community. Much discussion centred on the program mix, including technical and vocational training, university programs leading in the short term to associate degrees, as well as the possibility of having Aboriginal languages, or (fine) arts, or Aboriginal justice institutes. We talked about possible Cree names for the northern institution, as Cree was spoken by the majority of Aboriginal people in northern Manitoba. I found little interest in a Cree name, though we did brainstorm a number of possibilities. One important reason put forth for not using a Cree name was that there are other Aboriginal groups in the area, namely the Dene, Ojibway, and Métis. The northern post-secondary institution requested by the Keewatinook Okimahkanak (northern chiefs) had called for a University College of the North. It seemed appropriate to go with that name.

Our final report to the minister included several recommendations, the main one being that the proposed university college be a full degree-granting institution. There was unanimous rejection for associate degrees that would require students to complete their degrees at another institution that grants full degrees. Another recommendation, to reflect the Aboriginal reality and cultural diversity of the north, called for the establishment of a Centre for Aboriginal Studies and Research. It would be a vehicle through which

Aboriginal studies would be the foundation of learning for all students in all faculties, including those in trades, embedding Aboriginal knowledge throughout the curriculum. It would also be the hub of research on northern issues, an obvious benefit to the region, given the challenges confronting the north in terms of environment and development. It has always been my strong belief that everyone should have knowledge of the history of Aboriginal people and be aware of our progress and challenges over the years, as most everyone, regardless of their line of work, will at some time or another work for or alongside Aboriginal people.

I am pleased to have been a part of this historic and very important advancement in education for the people of northern Manitoba. The Minister of Advanced Education and Training, Hon. Diane McGifford, was as good as her word, to take the proposal for the new institution from debate to action. The University College of the North Act was passed in 2004, making the University College of the North a recognized entity of great importance to northerners.

As I was working on the proposal for the University College of the North, I recognized that if this new university was to reflect the Aboriginal reality and cultural diversity of the north, it needed to have Aboriginal professors. While there were a number of Aboriginal people with PhDs, they were all in demand and gainfully employed. It was apparent that this need had to be addressed. I had informal discussions with other interested friends and colleagues, and we came up with a list of Aboriginal people in Manitoba who had master's degrees. In all, we identified about 100 people who had their master's in various disciplines, though most were in education. From this base, we asked, how do we grow our own PhDs?

As I thought about this, I wondered with whom I could share this concern, preferably someone familiar with universities who would understand and appreciate the need and be able to help move it forward. I had been away from Manitoba for twenty-seven years, with the exception of the short interlude at Fisher River in 1979. I was not familiar with the current scene or the whereabouts of former colleagues. Then I remembered Deo Poonwassie, who had been a professor at the University of Manitoba for many years and had been instrumental in the success of the ACCESS program available to Aboriginal students.

We met for breakfast and I shared my concern with him and told him of my work at UBC to promote graduate studies for Aboriginal students. I wondered if a similar-style program could be initiated in Manitoba. The University of Manitoba was the logical university to approach, as it had a long-established program of graduate studies. This was not to say that the opportunity for Aboriginal students to pursue doctoral studies at the university were not always there, but my experience at UBC suggested that some sort of support system was essential to help our people navigate the system in higher education. I, personally, knew two people who had attempted doctoral studies at the University of Manitoba but became discouraged along the way. Cohorts have been a successful approach at all levels of study for our people. If we could interest ten to twenty eligible Aboriginal students to enter doctoral studies at the same time, they could act as supports to one another.

With this approach in mind, Deo and I met with the president of the university, Dr. Emőke Szathmáry. It was an easy sell, and I would later hear her say that she had thoughts along that line and was so happy with the idea that she almost kissed me. From there on, Deo and I met with the vice-president (academic) and provost to put together a plan. It was not a question of whether this should be done, but rather how to get it done.

In the meantime, I met with the dean of graduate studies to apprise him of the program in the works. I knew it would be beneficial if we could offer financial assistance to the students in the form of bursaries or scholarships, as this would be an incentive to students, especially those with families. While First Nations students can apply for band funding, it is usually insufficient to meet their needs. And since Métis students do not receive such government funding, I thought financial assistance would be a welcome incentive for them. The dean was impressed with the idea of the program. I suggested that we would be fundraising and that any financial help his department could provide would be an excellent way to show potential donors of the university's commitment. Without hesitation, he made a commitment of a sum of money over three years. This was a great beginning!

I then met with the university's director of Development and Advancement Services to discuss the program and the need to raise funds to assist the students. Once again, there was a favourable response, and she assigned a member of her staff to work with us. I wrote a proposal for funding and we began the process.

With advice from Deo and me, the dean struck a committee to direct and guide the program. The council members included the vice president of the University College of the North, a professor from the Native Studies department, a community person familiar with post-secondary education and Aboriginal people and organizations, the Dean of Graduate Studies and Deo and me. The program was named PhD Studies for Aboriginal Scholars (PSAS), and Deo became the coordinator on a half-time basis. We were set. The program was launched in 2007 with seven students.

Students in PSAS have exactly the same requirements as any student entering doctoral studies at the University of Manitoba. What is different is that they are part of a cohort model of delivery; that is, they are a part of a group who have common backgrounds, experiences, and interests who can give support to one another as they navigate through the system. Since they are in various faculties, they have designated times to meet as a cohort, arranged by the coordinator. It is a time when students can share information, seek input about their studies, or discuss challenges they are encountering. Peer support is very effective and adds strength to the program.

The fundraising was successful and over $1 million was raised, with a substantial sum coming from the university. We were then able to commit up to $20,000 per student per year for four years. Not all students take their allotment, as a number of them have secured grants from the Social Sciences and Humanities Research Council (SSHRC), a prestigious grant to receive, or scholarships and grants from other sources.

In 2012, we had two graduates from the program. Deo and I took part in the academic procession at graduation and acted like proud parents. Seeing a dream come true is very rewarding. There are another sixteen or so to graduate. These bright, enthusiastic PhD students have a vested interest in the advancement of Aboriginal people. This is reflected in the positions they hold and the research questions they pursue, as they search for answers to challenges faced by our people.

TOP TO BOTTOM

The Native Indian
Teacher Education
Program staff. Verna
(Supervisor), front row
second from right,
c. 1984.

The first Ts'kel gradua
(MEd), UBC, 1987:
Ethel Gardner, Francis
Johnson, Shirley Myra

FACING PAGE

Verna at the second
World Indigenous Peo
Conference in New
Zealand in 1990.

At my retirement party at UBC in 1993: Elder Minnie Croft, me, Mrs. Baker, Elder Simon Baker, Elder Vince Stogan, President David Strangway.

Receiving the Order of Canada, Ottawa, 1999. (Photo by Sgt. Christian Coulombe)

Receiving the Order of Manitoba, Winnipeg, 2007. (Photo by Tracey Goncalves)

Creating space for our people in the academic field seemed to be my forte. With Deo and the willing university personnel and interested Aboriginal scholars, this program became a reality in 2007 and has already begun to fill an obvious void. It was an honour to spend my time on such projects as a volunteer.

Of course, various activities I participated in overlapped during my retirement. I think it was rather coincidental that I was with three organizations during the same time—the National Aboriginal Achievement Foundation (NAAF), the Canadian Millennium Scholarship Foundation (CMSF), and the Helen Betty Osborne Memorial Foundation—all devoted to providing scholarships and bursaries to Aboriginal post-secondary students. In 1998, I was appointed to the board of the National Aboriginal Achievement Foundation (very recently renamed Indspire). The foundation has been in existence since 1985, its main purpose being to award scholarships and bursaries to post-secondary students across Canada. The foundation has attracted many sponsors and awarded millions of dollars since its inception. As of 2011–12, more than $6 million has been awarded to 2,220 individual recipients. During my nine years with the organization, I served on the executive, governance, program, and future directions committees. Most other committees dealt with finance, a very important area, as the foundation had to raise a lot of money for scholarships and bursaries.

In 1994, the foundation introduced the National Aboriginal Achievement Awards to recognize Aboriginal people who made outstanding contributions in the fields of business, community service, education, health, environment, justice, public service, spiritual leadership, sports, and lifetime achievement in any field. Since then, some categories have changed and several have been added, one of which is a youth award given to an outstanding student. Each year a gala is held to honour the recipients. The evening begins with a dinner followed by entertainment of the highest quality, showcasing Aboriginal performers. The gala, nationally televised, is our version of the Academy Awards and is a very special annual event. I received the National Aboriginal Achievement Award in 1994 for my work in education. Recipients are chosen by a nomination process and an independent jury makes the final selection.

While I was on the board, it occurred to me that we, the recipients, could serve a wider purpose than becoming board members and jurors for NAAF. With my mind on ways to advance Aboriginal education, I thought it would be a good idea to get the education laureates together to discuss ways in which Aboriginal education could be improved, given all that had taken place to date. Could we set a new direction? Knowing that each of the laureates had a clear knowledge of what had and is taking place in Aboriginal education, I saw this as an opportunity to think about a firm direction forward without spending a great deal of time rehashing what had already been done. We could be a springboard to future action.

I proposed to the board that we convene a meeting of the education laureates in a think-tank setting to discuss Aboriginal education. A motion was passed and plans were underway. First, a sponsor had to be found. I had previously met with a member of the Kenny Family Foundation, which was interested in assisting Aboriginal people. I submitted a proposal, and the foundation stepped forward to fund our venture.

Rather than having only the laureates meet, NAAF invited several laureates from other fields along with representatives from various Aboriginal organizations across the country. The group became quite large. The think tank was held at the First Nations Longhouse at UBC in September 2006. As is the tradition, two Elders from the Musqueam Nation were in attendance as well as the founders of the Kenny Family Foundation. While there was a healthy exchange of ideas over the course of two and a half days, we did not arrive at the kind of specific direction I had hoped for. Our report did contain several recommendations and it was presented to the Standing Committee on Aboriginal Affairs and Northern Development in September 2006. The report, *Policy Directions for Nurturing the Learning of Our People,* was made public online. Unfortunately, we did not make the impact with this effort that I had hoped for when the idea first occurred to me. I still think it would be good to get laureates together from various fields from time to time to discuss ways to move forward together in their respective fields. For example, I'm sure those in health would have many good ideas to deal with the growing health problems among our people. Since 2006, many more Aboriginal people have had their work recognized by NAAF and have received one of these prestigious awards.

In 1998, I was appointed to the Council of Members of the Canadian Millennium Scholarship Foundation (CMSF), a private, independent organization created by the Government of Canada to mark the new millennium. It was designed to provide scholarships and bursaries to post-secondary students across Canada, especially those facing economic barriers. The mission of the foundation was to distribute a $2.5 billion endowment over ten years. The Council of Members represented the Canadian public much like shareholders in a private corporation. One of our specific duties was to select a board that numbered fifteen in all, six of whom were government appointees. Our fifteen-member council was comprised of a diverse spectrum of Canadian society, representing every region, including college and university presidents, former premiers, educators, and students. I took it upon myself to ensure that there was Aboriginal representation on the board. We attended annual meetings and filled board vacancies when they occurred.

There was a great deal of change in the CMSF's knowledge and commitment to Aboriginal students from the time of its inception to the end of the ten years. At first, you heard little or no mention of Aboriginal people. As those of us involved on the board and council raised concerns, we alerted the foundation to take a greater interest in our people. The foundation undertook studies that brought to light the disparity in educational achievement between Aboriginal people and the Canadian public in general. Experimental programs were undertaken at the high school and university levels to promote access to and retention of Aboriginal students. Greater efforts were made to address the funding issue, and more and more Aboriginal students were awarded bursaries and scholarships. I was very pleased with the work of the foundation in general and was particularly impressed with how seriously it worked to address the Aboriginal situation. When the Conservative government did not renew the mandate after ten years, it was a very sad day for all Canadian students. The government announced that in its place they would create a Canada Student Grants Program with an initial $350 million to be operated by Human Resources and Skills Development Canada. For Aboriginal people, I felt this would mean that we would go back to the old days when everything in government for Aboriginal people got shuffled to the Department of Indian Affairs and Northern Development, which in turn shuffled all funding for students to the bands. The funding provided to bands for post-secondary education falls well short of the needs as more of our students become eligible for further studies.

I remained on the council for the duration of the foundation's term (2010). I felt that I played a part in bringing its focus onto Aboriginal education. In the book *A Million Futures: The Remarkable Legacy of the Canadian Millennium Foundation,* Silver Donald Cameron writes that the CMSF distributed more than a million scholarships and bursaries, a noteworthy achievement considering that there are only 34 million people in Canada.

The third bursary/scholarship foundation I was on was the Helen Betty Osborne Memorial Foundation (HBOMF). I was appointed to the board in 2003. Helen Betty was a young Aboriginal woman from Norway House who was murdered while she was in The Pas, Manitoba, pursuing her high school education with the goal of becoming a teacher. The Aboriginal Justice Inquiry of Manitoba concluded that her murder was marked by racism, sexism, and indifference. To pay tribute to her life, the Manitoba government created the foundation, which continues to assist Aboriginal students through bursaries and scholarships. The HBOMF was to raise funds to add to the contribution made by the provincial government.

One such effort was to have annual galas that included dinner and an auction, an event that also served to spotlight the work of the foundation. Each year an increasing number of students are assisted to continue their studies, thanks to the foundation. Since many more applications are received than can be provided for, an independent jury is in charge of the selection of candidates. From my experience with the National Aboriginal Achievement Foundation, I set up this jury system, as it distances the board members from any suspicion of partiality.

The HBOMF continues to serve the Aboriginal students of Manitoba who might not otherwise have had the opportunity to begin or continue their studies. In 2008, I was given a Champion Award by the foundation for lifetime achievement and advancement of Aboriginal people in post-secondary education.

Retirement is a splendid time, as it provides an opportunity to pick and choose your involvement based on those areas that are of most importance to you. I'm pleased with the many opportunities that have come my way and continue to keep me in the loop, albeit at a different pace as I age. I have talked about a number of these and will conclude with two more events that have a particular place in my memory.

In March 1997, I had the rare opportunity to go to Taiwan as the Canadian representative marking the 125th anniversary of the arrival in Taiwan of Dr. George Leslie MacKay, a Canadian missionary born in Ontario. The invitation had gone to a colleague of mine in Ontario who suggested I be invited. MacKay, who arrived in Taiwan in 1872, remained there until his death in 1901. He is remembered for learning the local language of Fukienese, building over 100 churches, and establishing Oxford College Seminary, Taiwan's first school for women, and the first hospital that bears his name. The Taiwanese have kept his memory alive for his exemplary contribution to health care, education, and helping women and Aboriginals access the education they deserved.

After an eleven-hour non-stop flight from Vancouver, I spent five whirlwind days in Taiwan. Taipei is a bustling city with traffic like I had never seen it before. Fortunately, I was escorted everywhere I went. I attended ceremonies at various locations where I gave short addresses. I didn't have much advance information on what was expected of me.

One day I flew to Aboriginal territory about a half-hour flight from Taiwan. Here, to my surprise, I was to give a two-day seminar at the Taiwan Theological Seminary, attended by clergymen from around the country who spoke only their native language. This meant that everything I said had to be translated. The sessions were long by our standards, going from 8:30 a.m. to 5:15 p.m. The topic I was to address on day one was Aboriginal Culture and on day two Aboriginal Education. Thankfully, these were two topics that were familiar to me, and while I did not have any prepared texts, I could speak to these areas. It was helpful to have ongoing translation, as this gave me time to think a step ahead.

A local man took me to see some ancient sights. On the way there, he stopped at a village and we went to talk to a man and two women who were sitting outside by a tent. He told them who I was and through his interpreting we had a brief conversation. I learned, to my surprise, that one of the women was ninety-nine years old. The other woman was her daughter. When we were about to leave, the ninety-nine-year-old woman asked if we wanted to see her mother. What? They took us in the house and there on the bed lay a 118-year-old woman, in a fetal position and looking very much like a baby, clean and very fragile.

My visit ended with another seminar of two hours at the Tamsui Oxford University College on "Preserving the Culture of Aboriginal People." Overall, this journey was a wonderful opportunity to experience yet another part of the world. I will remember this great honour for years to come and the contribution of Dr. George Leslie MacKay, a Canadian man, who spent his life helping the people of Taiwan.

Finally, one last story of having the privilege of being at a more recent event to mark the life and contribution of another great man, Robert W. Sterling, of the Nlaka'pamux Nation in the Merritt, BC, area. The invitation to attend came from the Nicola Valley Institute of Technology (NVIT) to attend the official naming of their library in memory of Robert Sterling. The family of Robert had asked NVIT to invite me because I had been a close colleague and friend of his through my work as NITEP supervisor. Robert had been instrumental in much of the early progress made at UBC, particularly as he was one of the founders of NITEP and its committee chair since its inception. Along with a few other Aboriginal students in university in the sixties, they were the first to make an impact on addressing Native Indian education at UBC. I was invited to be one of the speakers at the ceremony.

I was certainly pleased to share a short message on behalf of my old friend. I spoke of when I first met Robert when he came as a BC delegate and Elder to one of our conferences in Manitoba. I expected to meet a much older person, and here was this freckle-faced, red-haired man, younger than me, who was an Elder. It didn't take long for me to see why he came in that capacity; his knowledge and ways of presenting were befitting an Elder. Whatever role I saw him in, in the years to follow, he expressed the same depth and charm as he had when I first met him—he was an extraordinary person.

I mentioned, as well, how I have often quoted Robert's last address to a graduating class. Here are the last lines of his profound address:

I have learned:

Not just to look – but to see!

Not just to touch – but to feel!

Not just to take steps – but to stride!

Not just to listen – but to hear!

Not just to talk – but to say something!

Not just to dream – but to do something!

Not just to take – but to give!

Not just to exist – but to be!

If life in the future seems to challenge me, change me, depend on me, use me, hurt me, laugh at me, criticize me, tempt me, complicate me,

Then I am ready!!!

We are trained – but are we ready?

There is a powerful lesson in those words, and they still inspire me to take what I have learned and do what I can to support the Aboriginal community.

CHAPTER SEVEN

Leaving Vancouver

JUST AS I GAVE LITTLE THOUGHT as to what I would do after I retired from UBC at age fifty-seven, I did not consider whether I would leave Vancouver and move elsewhere. I loved Vancouver—the mountains, the ocean, the beaches. I lived in four different places in Kitsilano over nearly twenty years. I wasn't just practising my nomadic ancestry by moving so often: I always had a good reason. First I rented a one-bedroom apartment, then a duplex with a room for my nephew while he lived with me, then I bought a one-bedroom condo. When I retired I found I needed a home office space so I bought a one-bedroom condo with a den. At each place I was within walking distance of Kitsilano or Jericho Beach. I loved going for walks or just sitting at the beach looking out on the water and to West Vancouver on the other side of English Bay.

When I rented the duplex with a big backyard, I quite often had barbeques for our students, and in winter we would gather in the house to enjoy the lovely fireplace and a stir-fry dinner. Just as they had to do their own barbequing, they had to do their own cooking. I had everything ready, the meat and various vegetables. The last birthday gift my mother and dad had given me was a large wok. This came in handy, not only for our stir-fries, but also for warming large quantities of chilli at the NITEP hut. I was sorry to leave the house when the owners decided to sell it. It was way out of my price range. That is when I decided to buy a condo. My new condo had one bedroom with a beautiful patio on the ground floor, all fenced in with red rhododendrons that bloomed brilliantly during the spring months. My last condo, with more space, was within walking distance to the beach and to Granville Market. I was happy with each of the places where I lived.

Shortly after I got to Vancouver, I took up cross-country skiing. My friend Peg was an avid skier at the time. Her other skiing friends and I would often go to Cypress Mountain. Believe it or not, it was about a half-hour from where I lived. I crossed the Lion's Gate Bridge to the north shore and headed west, and there it was. We even went to Whistler to ski. What is called cross-country skiing in BC is really quite steep. You could get on a trail on Cypress and go for a kilometre. So you had to learn how to slow down and stop. I never took any lessons so I remained an amateur. At Whistler Mountain, I resorted to skiing with the children on the bunny hill. The kids were really good to me. They were fun.

I had the privilege of another wonderful West Coast experience, travelling in a sailboat. Peg and her friend owned a boat that could sleep four people. She also had an Airedale dog named Shandy that went on these trips. She had to take Shandy to shore in the dinghy several times to do her business. When my nephew lived with me he came on a few boating trips. He sure found it funny to see this big dog being taken to shore in a wee dinghy. We cooked our meals on the boat and enjoyed our morning coffee on the deck. The most memorable part of the boating trips was the time we spent in Desolation Sound. The name does not do it justice; it is one of the most scenic places I have ever seen. Often, on these boating trips, we would anchor the boat and go to shore for a walk, or if there were shops we would browse around. We set crab traps and ate fresh crab or we fished and ate fresh salmon. We sometimes treated ourselves to a meal in a restaurant.

We had strange incidents, as well, such as the time we were anchored to a log boom and woke up when the log boom began to move. When you are on a sailboat, it is not as glamorous as it is sometimes portrayed; you have to work hard. It takes two people to operate the boat, though I have known of people to go solo. You have to keep adjusting the sails, and keep steering the proper way into the wind. To change directions you have to "come about," which means switching the sail entirely, and you must be careful not to get hit by the boom. Landing at docks was not always an easy matter either, particularly if it was windy. You had to jump off the boat and quickly wrap the rope around a part of the dock. We managed to have a few bruises and cuts and scrapes. All in all, I wouldn't have traded this experience for the world.

Another reason I loved Vancouver was the golfing. The season was much longer than we get in the prairies. My friend, Don, helped me select clubs and taught me the game. I loved it! He took me to many golf courses, each one having a beauty of its own. We would enjoy a cool glass of beer after a game or go for lunch or dinner depending on when we were playing.

So why would anyone leave all this? I retired in 1993 and left in 1999. Jim and I had kept in touch over all the years after I left Ottawa. We took holidays together to places like Puerto Vallarta, Las Vegas, Reno, Oregon, Cuba, and Florida. I read somewhere that there is a name for people with the arrangement we have: LAT, living apart together. That's about how it was, and how it still is. In 1999, Jim was still the live-in manager at Cedar Cove Resort. And he, his brother, and I were still co-owners. My shares in the company were minimal because I did not continue to put money toward it after I left Ottawa. I spent some time at Cedar Cove every year. Jim had put on a big party for me in April 1999 when I received the Order of Canada. My family members from Fisher River, Thunder Bay, Petrolia, Sault Ste. Marie, and Toronto were invited to spend the weekend with us. They stayed in the cottages and took their meals in the restaurant at the lodge. It was a wonderful time. One of the gifts I received was a double eagle feather, which is very rare. To receive it was a great honour.

Jim and I were considering building a house near the property. We walked through the bush several times, looking at a number of possible sites. We had more or less settled on a spot when a house he had built at the edge of the property for a couple that worked for him became vacant. We decided we would take over the vacated house and have a sunroom built on the side facing the marsh and water. We would finish the basement to have a family room and a guest room. I planned the big move for October of that year. I had mixed feelings about this, as Vancouver had been my home for so long and I had many friends there. I'm the kind of person who likes to share what I am doing with others. Surprising, even to me, I kept this impending move quiet. I finally told three of my closest friends, separately, and they were devastated with the news. There was no turning back: I had made a decision. What was my decision based on? It is hard to tell. I was financially secure and in good health, but I was preparing to settle in and share my old age with Jim. Just before I left, I put on my own farewell party in the social room of my building. My invitation was my way of letting my colleagues and friends know that I was leaving. Most everyone I invited came by to wish me well. They were able to meet Jim, some of them for the first time. Many were unaware of my ties to him. I had my furniture transported to Cedar Cove, about ninety kilometres west of Ottawa. Jim had flown out, so we drove back together, visiting friends along the way. We knew people in Alberta, Saskatchewan (where his sister lives), Winnipeg, Thunder Bay, Sault Ste. Marie. We took our time travelling east.

Our house renovations were not completed, but we moved into the house anyway. The move was a change for Jim as well. He had been living in a suite in the lodge ever since we bought the place in 1978, with his living quarters shrinking as the facilities in the lodge expanded. He was happy to have a house once again.

Okay, so here I am at Cedar Cove, retired, ready to carve out a new life. At that point, my mind was set on writing and thought that would be it. No more of the other things I used to work on. I was retired. I would continue to work on the boards of the National Aboriginal Achievement Foundation and the Canadian Millennium Scholarship Foundation, both of which I joined in 1998. It was quiet for a few months until people began to find out where I was living. Then came requests to speak here and there, the panels, the travel, and I began all over again, but at a much slower pace. This was fine. Jim, on the other hand, was very busy managing the resort, as he did in the past. Most days he was out the door at 6:30 a.m., back for lunch, and back for dinner. After dinner, he visited his mother, who lived on the resort in a comfortable cottage Jim had built for her after his father died in 1980. Quite often, he went back to his office to do paper work after that. This occurred seven days a week with only the odd exception. He was just doing what he had been doing for many years. I soon realized that if this kept up it might be a rather lonely existence. I had lived in Ottawa in the 1970s, but found that my friends had all moved on and things were not the same. I did have a friend in Kingston, but that was not exactly nearby. I kept house and cooked more than I was used to doing. Jim is a good cook, and he often came back in time to help with dinner. We usually had our glass of wine. We did have some of his friends over for dinner now and again, at which time Jim was in charge of cooking. I was what they called a "bull cook" or "cookie" out on Lake Winnipeg, peeling potatoes and generally getting everything ready for the chef. On special occasions such as Thanksgiving, Easter, and Christmas we usually hosted the dinner for family and friends. I did have a nephew and his wife who worked at Cedar Cove. They had two children. It was great to have some time with them, even babysitting on occasion. Several friends and relatives from around the country, especially my friends from Vancouver, came to spend a few days with us. It was wonderful to have the company.

One of my daily routines was to visit Jim's mother Ruth, usually in the late afternoon. Sometimes we would walk to the lodge and have a drink. She liked her brandy, and I usually had wine. As she began to lose her sight, she spent hours listening to talking books, mainly biographical in nature. She did not like fiction. Mrs. Wright lived into her nineties. She had a degree, which was rare for women of her day. When she had us over for dinner, I helped her prepare it. She taught me the best way to prepare pork tenderloin. She loved to tell me stories of her life as a girl—a rather naughty girl, she thought. She was great company, and if I did any good while I lived there, it would be that I could be her companion for some time most every day.

Jim and I went away each winter for a month or two. Florida was the place of choice since it was straight south of us and a place that Jim liked. We spent time in Florida, even before I moved to Cedar Cove, and had stayed at various places. The two years I was with him in Ontario, we spent our time at St. Pete Beach. I have a cousin, Link, and his wife, Reta, in Dryden, who go there every year for three months, from January to early April. It was good to be near them; we could get together for meals, eating in or out. My cousin is a great one for clipping coupons, and we often ate at places with good discounts, thanks to his coupons. We went out for a special dinner on Jim's birthday in January. When Jim had a balloon hat made for him, it was almost too much—we couldn't stop laughing.

I loved living in a house in a quiet spot, free of traffic noises. I had never had a house to call my own. At least it felt like our own, though technically it belonged to the Cedar Cove Resort (which was us) and, according to our by-laws, we were required to pay rent, as the previous couple had done. My favourite area was the sun room. We had windows all across the side facing the water, and, with a fireplace, it was a cozy room to spend time, especially in the winter. We often took our meals there instead of in the dining room. Jim had a beautiful antique dining room suite that could seat up to twelve comfortably. It served us well when we had a large group over. Much of my time was spent in the big den, working on my computer or playing games. Jim had put up a bird house just outside my window, and I could watch the birds there. We had hammocks in the yard, though I was the only one who used them. Our patio extended around two sides of the house. It was very comfortable.

I took on the responsibility of doing the grocery shopping in the nearby town of Arnprior. This is where our doctor and dentists were located. We purchased most of what we needed there. For restaurant food and supplies, Jim went to a wholesaler in Ottawa. I sometimes went to a movie in Kanata, about a half-hour from where we lived. There were times when I accompanied Jim to Ottawa, and we would go for dinner, usually East Indian food, which we both really enjoy, or we would go to the casino and have dinner there. Jim did not like to gamble but came with me and waited while I tried my luck for a couple of hours. He would spend ten dollars. He would put money into a machine and if it paid him anything he would put it in his pocket until his original ten dollars was all gone.

I was able to spend time on my writing and went off to various places in response to invitations. It was good to be in touch. I guess the saying "once a teacher, always a teacher" could apply to me. Education has had a pivotal place in my life, and continuing to be involved was good for me, though I did think I could leave it behind. Being on my own much of the time at Cedar Cove was not what I expected. I began to find this all very stressful. It showed that I did not take everything into consideration when I made the move. I was retired, and Jim wasn't. I need friends to do things with, and to share things with, and it wasn't happening. Though I was used to living alone, as was Jim, I had expectations of spending much more time together.

Being alone really got to me, and I began to feel sick and realized that it was stress, which was confirmed by my doctor. Finally, after a few discussions with Jim about our situation, I could see that this was not going to work. As long as he was in charge of Cedar Cove Resort, things were not going to change. Obviously, we were still not ready to be together and probably never would be. I began to think of moving away. Where? Back to Vancouver? No, "been there, done that," as they say. Besides, to move back after selling my condo would be financially unwise and virtually impossible.

It was during this time that I was invited to the first Aboriginal reunion at the University of Manitoba. I attended an evening dinner and was one of the speakers. It was great to meet old friends again. Elijah Harper, Ovide Mercredi, and Moses Okemow were present. They were all university students when I was the education director at the Manitoba Indian Brotherhood in the 1970s. They made their mark at the university (as they made their mark later in life) by forming the Indian, Métis, and Eskimo Student Association at the University of Manitoba, the precursor of the current Aboriginal Students Association.

When it was my turn to speak, I recalled my first experience at the university. I told the audience that my transcript begins with an "F." I joked that I thought I had done well and that "F" meant fabulous. Of course, I'm well aware of why I failed that geography class, and it simply adds up to not taking it seriously and studying. Teachers' college (normal school) had been a breeze, so I treated this course that same way. I was young, engaged, and having a great social life. It was the wrong time to pursue university studies. In fact, I did not try again until years later.

I had decided that on this trip I would go to Fisher River to ask my brother, Reggie, if I could build a house on his property. I had called my sister and asked her to invite him to dinner at their place, as I had something to discuss with them. In the meantime, the morning after the reunion event, I was having breakfast by myself and reading the *Winnipeg Free Press*. I reached the section advertising houses and condos. Something struck me about a place called Marina del Rey, where there was a condo for sale. As I thought about it, I remembered that this was where Pat, a friend of mine, lived. I also remembered that she would be back from Hawaii, where she spends her winters. It was May, and I decided to phone her. She came over to join me, and I told her my story. She and her husband had lived in this building for years and she told me that it was well kept and they had just repaired the roof. She urged me to call the gentleman selling the condo before I went to Fisher River. I did that, and he came by to show it to me. It was a two-bedroom condo, over 1,100 square feet, with underground parking. The last one I owned in Vancouver was less than 900 square feet, and this one would cost half as much. I told him I was interested and would he wait until noon tomorrow for a definite answer. I think I knew then that I would take it. While I had not been considering Winnipeg, it would be a wise move. Pat, now a widow, was pleased that I might move in. We could resume our old friendship—we had known each other since the Norway House days in the 1960s. She also reminded me that since I still travelled a fair bit, living in Winnipeg would be much more convenient.

I drove to Fisher River that same day. Supper was ready, and Reggie was there. I asked if they were curious about why I wanted to talk to them. Darlene replied tearfully, "You're moving to New Zealand." She knew how much I loved New Zealand and that I had many friends there. She was relieved to know that wasn't it. Reggie said, "You're getting married." Well, it was quite the opposite. Then my brother-in-law, George, piped up, "You're moving home." I went on to explain that it had been my intention to ask Reggie if I could build a house on his property and move back to Fisher River, but having found a condo in Winnipeg, I had a change of plans. Reggie said that I was very welcome to build right by the river, a spot that still had my mom and dad's old house, which he now used as a warehouse. The warehouse could be moved, and I could take the spot where there were lovely trees that my dad had planted when Reggie was barely walking. It would have been ideal. But the next morning I called the fellow selling the condo and told him I would take it. I arranged to meet him to work out the details. I could take possession in July. I called Jim to tell him the news. It was a great surprise to him; he did not know I planned to leave. It was a done deal. I may not have handled this right, but I had made a decision. I rented a U-Haul, and my nephew drove it out to Winnipeg in late June. We arrived on a weekend, so we did not have to return the truck until Monday. Dennis, being a journeyman painter, suggested that he paint the two bedrooms before we moved the furniture in. We stayed at Pat's in the meantime.

Jim and I had an amicable parting, but I didn't call him nor did he call me for months. It was when his mother passed away that we reunited. He was devastated. I had known her well and it was a loss for me as well. He was good to his mother, as were his siblings. I accompanied him to the funeral in Saskatoon. From then on, we resumed our relationship in much the same way we had done the previous thirty-some years.

Upon Reflection

I BELIEVE IN DIVINE GUIDANCE. I returned to live at Fisher River for a brief time in 1979–80 when I had been asked by the Band to come to work with them as they planned to take control of education in Fisher River. I talked about this earlier. The job did not turn out, but one could assume that my real purpose in returning was to spend my dad's last days with him and to see my mother through her cancer ordeal that took her life within a year of my dad's passing. I am grateful for that time I had with them.

Similarly, I returned in 2001, and sadly have laid to rest my youngest brother, Reggie, my nephew, David, who was raised by my parents, my step-brother Clarence, and just two years ago my younger sister, Darlene. Several other relatives have also passed on during these past twelve years. Again, I give thanks that I was led home to enjoy some time with my family.

I am happy being where I am. Living in Winnipeg in a condominium where I have many friends means everything to me. It is a comfortable and safe place to be. My cousin Pat moved here over a year ago. She has an apartment on the fifth floor. It seems that much more like home when you have family nearby.

It is now 2013 and I find it hard to believe that I have been officially retired nearly twenty years. I just had my seventy-seventh birthday. Thankfully, I am well and have no difficulty driving around. I have been blessed with good health all my life. I did have a setback as I suffered from arthritis in my hips. I wondered how that could happen, since I am generally very active. I spent a lot of time at the indoor swimming pools in Vancouver. I walked to the beaches and through the parks. As a youngster at home, I often won races; I played baseball and skated. In high school I curled. I love sports. To this day my friends know there is no point in calling me or dropping in for a visit if the Winnipeg Blue Bombers or the Winnipeg Jets are playing. The BC Lions are still one of my favourite teams and I am also a fan of the Toronto Blue Jays and try not to miss any major curling bonspiels. All of this is on television, of course.

I would say that I am still an active person. In 2009, I had my right hip replaced and in 2010, I had my left hip done. I have since begun to golf again. I am fortunate to have been afflicted with something that could be corrected. Being able to move around freely has given me a new lease on life.

So what would I do differently if I were to live my life over again? Well, not much. I am comfortable with my destiny. I wonder about whether I would be happier if I had married and had a family. Maybe, maybe not! I have nieces and nephews with families and a number of my friends' children who call me auntie. I am an "adopted" grandma of several lovely people. I am surrounded by wonderful people—relatives, friends, colleagues, former students, and former classmates—and then there is my faithful friend Jim. In a way, I still have it all.

I am grateful to the Creator for the interesting life I have had and continue to enjoy. It has truly been rewarding to delve more deeply into education and to have been, as Tennyson writes, "a part of all that I have met." What took me from a one-room classroom to one of the largest universities in Canada, I can only classify as an opportunity to create space for our people in academia. Doors, challenges, just kept opening up for me, and I am richer for all who I have had the privilege of working for and working with over the last fifty-eight years. It delights me to see the growing number of Aboriginal people who are taking their places in all walks of life and levels of society. We will make a difference. We are making a difference. While it may sometimes feel that progress is not happening fast enough, we have to remind ourselves that we have only in the last fifty to sixty years begun to actively deal with hundreds of years of colonialism. The pace of progress and healing will accelerate as the impact of our numbers in the workplace increases, and not in my lifetime but in the near future, the change will be clearly evident.

Having begun my story by revealing that I do not know who my biological father is, I do know who I am. I am, first and foremost, a Cree woman. It is my identity. The fact that I was born out of wedlock, have been a non-Status Indian, a Status Indian, a Métis (if we define this as being of mixed blood), and adopted, I have not allowed myself to be defined by any of these labels. Rather, my life has unfolded in a relatively uncomplicated way. Yes, I am a Cree woman and I'm a passionate and optimistic person. It is my hope that this effort will inspire others to tell their stories. It is one way to record history.

Ekosi, Ke-nuna'skomitin-awow. I thank you for having taken the time to read my story.

APPENDIX 1
AWARDS AND HONOURS

2012 Honorary Doctor of Cannon Law, St. John's College, University of Manitoba

2012 Queen's Diamond Jubilee Medal

2011 Honorary Faculty Member, Nicola Valley Institute of Technology

2009 Verna J. Kirkness Education Foundation – named in her honour

2008 Honorary Doctor of Laws, University of Manitoba

2008 Verna J. Kirkness "Be a Food Researcher for a Week" Youth Initiative

2008 Champion Award, Helen Betty Osborne Memorial Foundation

2007 The Order of Manitoba, Winnipeg

2004 Nomination for YMCA/YWCA Women of Distinction Award

2003 Queen's Golden Jubilee Medal

2002 Aboriginal Women in Leadership Distinction Award, First Nations Training and Consulting Services National Steering Committee

2002 Verna J. Kirkness Institute of Higher Learning – honoured by the Fisher River Education Authority

2001 Listed, *Canadian Who's Who* (Vol. 36)

2000 Named 24th of "The Best 50 British Columbia Thinkers"

1998 Member of the Order of Canada

1994–95 Listed, *World's Who's Who of Women* (12th edition)

1994 Honorary Doctor of Laws, University of British Columbia

1994 National Aboriginal Achievement Award

1994 Associate Professor Emerita, University of British Columbia

1992 The Commemorative Medal for 125th Anniversary of Confederation

1992 Honorary Doctor of Laws, University of Western Ontario

1990 UBC 75th Anniversary Medal

1990 UBC Alumni Award

1990 Honorary Doctor of Humane Letters, Mount St. Vincent University

1990 Canadian Educator of the Year Award, Canadian "Youth Education" Excellence Prize

1990 British Columbia Educator of the Year Award

1990 Appreciation Award, St. Theresa Point Education Authority

1988 Fellow of the Ontario Institute of Studies in Education

1988 Gold Eagle Feather Award, BC Professional Native Women's Association

1987 President Emerita, Mokakit Indian Education Research Association

1985 Honorary Graduate, Native Indian Teacher Education Program, UBC

1984 Kirkness Adult Learning Centre – honoured by its Board of Directors

EAGLE FEATHERS

Over the course of my career I have received ten Eagle Feathers. When an eagle feather is given it is an indication that the community believes the person it is given to has the vision of an eagle to see far and to have the courage and strength to carry out their responsibilities. Eagle feathers are usually given in recognition of accomplishments. This is the highest honour that Aboriginal people give in recognition of achievement.

APPENDIX 2

BIBLIOGRAPHY OF SELECTED PUBLICATIONS

Books and Book Chapters

2012   Kirkness, Verna J. "Foreword." In *Living Indigenous Leadership: Native Narratives on Building Strong Communities*, ed. Carolyn Kenny and Tina Ngaroimata Fraser. Vancouver: UBC Press.

2001   Kirkness, Verna J., and Ray Barnhardt. "First Nations and Higher Education: The Four R's—Respect, Relevance, Reciprocity, Responsibility." In *Education Across Cultures: A Contribution to Dialogue Among Civilizations*. Hong Kong: Comparative Education Research Centre, University of Hong Kong. Published in English and Chinese.

2001   Kirkness, Verna J., and Jo-ann Archibald. *The First Nations Longhouse: Our Home Away from Home*. Vancouver: UBC Press.

1999   Kirkness, Verna J., ed. *O Great Creator: A Collection of Works by Ruth Elizebeth (Bette) Spence*. Self-published.

1998   Kirkness, Verna J. *Aboriginal Languages: A Collection of Talks and Papers*. Self-published.

1994   Kirkness, Verna J., ed. *Khot-La-Cha: The Autobiography of Chief Simon Baker*. Vancouver: Douglas and McIntyre.

1993   Kirkness, Verna J., and Ray Barnhardt. "First Nations and Higher Education: The Four R's—Respect, Relevance, Reciprocity, Responsibility." In *Knowledge Across Cultures: Universities East and West*. Wuhan, China: Hubei Education Press; Toronto: OISIE Press. Published in English, French, and Chinese.

1992   Kirkness, Verna J., and Sheena Selkirk Bowman. *First Nations and Schools: Triumphs and Struggles*. Toronto: Canadian Education Association. Published in English and French.

1992   Kirkness, Verna J. "The First Nations House of Learning: A Case of Successful Transformation." In *Beyond Multicultural Education: International Perspectives*, ed. Kogila A. Moodley. Calgary: Detselig Enterprises.

1986   Kirkness, Verna, J. "Indian Control of Indian Education: Over a Decade Later." In *Selected Papers from the First Mokakit Conference: Establishing Pathways to Excellence in Indian Education*, ed. Harvey A. McCue. Vancouver: Mokakit Indian Education Research Association.

1984   Kirkness, Verna J. *Indians of the Plains*. Toronto: Grolier.

1983   Kirkness, Verna J. "Walk in Our Moccasins." In *First People, First Voices*, ed. Penny Petrone. Toronto: University of Toronto Press.

1978   Kirkness, Verna J. *Education of Indians in Federal and Provincial Schools in Manitoba*. Ottawa: Department of Indian and Northern Affairs.

1976   Kirkness, Verna J. *Manitoba Native Bilingual Program: A Handbook*. Ottawa: Department of Indian Affairs and Northern Development, Ottawa

1975   Kirkness, Verna J. "Special Report: Canada's Native Indian People." *Encyclopedia Britannica*, 1975 Yearbook.

1974   Kirkness, Verna J. "Foreword." In *Wild Drums: Tales and Legends of the Plains Indians as Told to Nan Shipley*, by Alex Grisdale. Winnipeg: Peguis Publishers.

1973   Sealey, D. Bruce, and Verna J. Kirkness, eds. *Indians Without Tipis: A Resouce Book*. Winnipeg: W. Clare.

Articles in Journals

2001   Kirkness, Verna J. "Aboriginal Education in Canada: A Retrospective and a Prospective." *Our Schools, Our Selves* 10, 3. 97–121.

1999   Kirkness, Verna J. "Aboriginal Education in Canada: A Retrospective and Prospective." *Journal of American Indian Education* 39, 1. 14–30.

1998   Kirkness, Verna J., "Our People's Education: Cut the Shackles, Cut the Crap, Cut the Mustard." *Canadian Journal of Native Education* 22, 1. 10–15.

1998   Kirkness, Verna J. "The Critical State of Aboriginal Languages in Canada." *Canadian Journal of Native Education* 22, 1. 93–107.

1995   Kirkness, Verna J. "Aboriginal Peoples and Tertiary Education in Canada: Institutional Responses." *London Journal of Canadian Studies* 11 (Special Issue – Aboriginal Peoples). 28–41

1992   Kirkness, Verna J. "First Nations House of Learning Promotes Maori Language Immersion Model." *Multiculturalism* 16, 2/3. 64–67.

1991   Kirkness, Verna J., and Ray Barnhardt. "First Nations and Higher Education: The Four R's—Respect, Relevance, Reciprocity, Responsibility." *Journal of American Indian Education* 30, 3. 1–15.

1989   Kirkness, Verna J. "Aboriginal Languages Foundation: A Mechanism for Renewal." *Canadian Journal of Native Education* 16, 2. 25–41.

1988   Kirkness, Verna J. "The Power of Language in Determining Success." *TESL Manitoba Journal* 5, 2. 1–7.

1987   Kirkness, Verna J. "Teaching Indian Languages." *Journal of Indigenous Studies* 1, 2. 97–103.

1987   Kirkness, Verna J. "Emerging Native Women." *Canadian Journal of Women and the Law* 2, 2. 408–415

1987   Kirkness, Verna J. "Indian Education: Past, Present and Future." *Aurora: The Professional Journal of the NWT Teachers* 5, 1. 19–26.

1987 McEachern, William, and Verna J. Kirkness. "Teacher Education for Aboriginal Groups: One Model and Suggested Application." *Journal of Education for Teaching* 13, 2. 133–144.

1986 Kirkness, Verna J. "Native Indian Teachers: A Key to Progress." *Canadian Journal of Native Education* 13, 1. 47–53.

1984 Kirkness, Verna J. "Native Languages: Confusion and Uncertainty." *Networks – TESL Canada.* 5–6.

1983 Kirkness, Verna J. "Native Teacher Education Programs in Canada." *Laurentian University Review* 25, 2. 83–86.

1981 Kirkness, Verna J. "The Education of Canadian Indian Children." *Child Welfare League of America* 60, 7. 447–455.

1977 Kirkness, Verna J., "Prejudice about Indians in Textbooks." *Journal of Reading* 20, 7. 595–600.

1976 Kirkness, Verna J. "Programs for Native People by Native People." *Education Canada* 16, 4. 32–35.

APPENDIX 3

ARCHIVAL COLLECTIONS AT THE UNIVERSITY OF BRITISH COLUMBIA

First Nations House of Learning, Xwi7xwa Archives
Kirkness, Verna J. (1972–2006). *Speeches, Publications and Papers series.* Verna J. Kirkness fonds (XA-2, Box 1-3). University of British Columbia, Xwi7xwa Library, Vancouver, BC.

Verna J. Kirkness – cIRcle
Kirkness, Verna J. (1972–2006). *Verna J. Kirkness Speeches.* cIRcle: UBC's Digital Repository: Xwi7xwa Library, Aboriginal Education , Verna J. Kirkness Speeches 1974–2000. Available at https://circle.ubc.ca/handle/2429/29911.

University of British Columbia Archives
Kirkness, Verna J. (1964–2009). Verna J. Kirkness fonds (Box 1). University of British Columbia Archives. Vancouver, BC. Finding aid available at http://www.library.ubc.ca/archives/u_arch/kirkness.pdf.

Memory BC, University of British Columbia Archives, Verna J. Kirkness Fonds
University of British Columbia Archives. (2012, March 16). *Verna J. Kirkness fonds.* Available at http://memorybc.ca/verna-j-kirkness-fonds.

INDEX

24, 41, 97; and Master Tuition Agreement, 70–72; and negotiations over Indian Act, 83–84; as source of Native funding, 65, 115; VK does consultancy work for, 89–91

Indian Control of Indian Education (paper), 74–75, 90

Indian Control of Indian Education (policy): attempt at Fisher River, 93–97; and negotiation of Indian Act, 83–84; and NIB, 78; and parental responsibility, 90; policy paper on implementation, 79–82; VK workshops on, 101

Indian Medical Services, 42

Indians of Canada, 73

Indians Without Tipis (Sealey and Kirkness), 77

J

James Bay and Northern Quebec Agreement, 88

Jasper, Ken, 50, 51, 58

Johnson, Francis, 121

Johnson, Keith, 34

Jones, Dudley, 38

Jones, Jennifer, 157

Joseph, Gene, 118, 119

K

Kawagley, Oscar, 150

Keeper, Joe, 77

Kenny Family Foundation, 164

Khot-La-Cha: The Autobiography of Simon Baker (Kirkness), 154

Khot La Cha Award, 154

King, Cecil, 137, 138

Kirkness, Annie, 9

Kirkness, Clarence, 7, 8, 179

Kirkness, Darlene: birth, 8; caring for her mother, 103, 104; at Cedar Cove Park, 92; death, 179; living with VK, 97; and mother's funeral, 105; and VK's move to Winnipeg, 176, 177

Kirkness, Evelyn, 29

Kirkness, Fred: death, 97; and death of children, 7–8; good works of, 104–5; married life, 7, 11–12; relationship

with VK, 5, 16, 39, 51–52, 106–7; and travel, 85, 86

Kirkness, Gladys Mae, 8

Kirkness, Gloria, 108

Kirkness, Ida, 7, 16, 23

Kirkness, Margaret, 7, 8

Kirkness, Maria (VK's grandmother), 8

Kirkness, Maria Jane (VK's sister), 7

Kirkness, Mary Ann, 6, 8, 15, 25, 26, 103, 104, 125

Kirkness, Mooshoom "Jim", 8–9

Kirkness, Pamela, 105–6

Kirkness, Reggie: birth, 8; at Cedar Cove Park, 92; death, 179; and mother's death, 104, 106; and VK's graduation, 16; and VK's move to Winnipeg, 176, 177

Kirkness, Rosalie, 49–50

Kirkness, Rosalyn, 7–8

Kirkness, Verna: achieves tenure at UBC, 119–20; birth, 6; building UBC longhouse, 145–51, 155; and *Canadian Journal of Native Education,* 137–38; closeness to extended family, 6, 7, 8–10, 49–50, 110–11; as co-chair of President's Ad Hoc Committee, 125–28; creating curriculum for Natives, 59–61, 66; as cross-cultural educational consultant, 61, 62–66; as director of First Nations House of Learning, 128–34; early jobs of, 16; early school years, 3–5, 12–14, 15, 16–17; as education director of MIB, 67, 68, 69–70, 72–73; as education director of NIB, 77–82, 83; and education takeover at Fisher River, 93–97; effect of being a non-Status Indian on, 10, 12, 17, 125; establishing University College of the North, 157–63; foundation work, 163–66, 173; as freelance education consultant, 86–87, 89–91, 97, 99, 101–2; growing up in Fisher River, 10–12; and her mom's death, 102–7; hired as supervisor of NITEP, 98–101; hobbies of, 111, 171–72, 180; interest in politics, 87–89; legally changes name, 28; life in Cedar Cove, 172–76; life in Norway House, 36–39; life in Vancouver, 170–72; life in Winnipeg, 176–80; and Manitoba Native Bilingual Program, 63–66; and Mokakit Indian Education Research Association, 133, 134–37; opening tenure track to Natives, 132–33; organizes World Conference of Indigenous People, 138–39; as parliamentary research assistant, 87–89; pride in being Cree, 25, 107–8, 181; public speaking by, 44–45, 54, 75, 81, 113, 116, 124, 156, 176; receives teacher training, 18–20, 22–23, 24; reflections on her life, 179–81; as representative in Taiwan, 167–68; research into language initiatives, 139–43; retirement from UBC, 151–52, 153, 156; as student counsellor in Winnipeg, 41–45; study on anti-Indian bias in textbooks, 72–73; as supervisor of NITEP, 109–10, 112–19, 121; as supervisor of schools at Frontier, 50–61; takes university courses, 75–76, 87, 89, 91, 96, 176; teaches at Bellhampton, 20–22; teaches at Birtle Indian Residential School, 29–33; teaches at Fisher River, 23, 24–28, 29; teaches at Rossville Residential School, 34–36, 38–40; teaches with NITEP, 100, 107–9, 119; travel, 46–48, 61–62, 84–86; tributes and honours, 150, 152, 163, 166, 172; as visiting professor, 156–57; work for Fairford Indian band, 97; work on Aboriginal Languages Institute, 143–45; writing of, 69–70, 77, 82, 112, 119–20, 129, 154–55, 175, 177

Klesner, Peg, 101–2, 108, 117, 171

Kohanga Reo, 140–43

L

languages. See Native languages, preservation of

Lawrence, Dana, 115–16

Linklater, Clive, 77–78, 80, 86, 109

Longhouse at UBC, 145–51, 155

Louis, Kathy, 149

Lund, Loreen, 45

M

MacIvor, Madeleine, 129, 131

Mack, Sharon, 120

MacKay, George Leslie, 167, 168

Manitoba, Government of, 62–66, 157–60, 166

Manitoba: Its Peoples and Places, 73

Manitoba Indian Brotherhood (MIB), 67–70

Manitoba Native Bilingual Program, 63–66

Manuel, George, 74, 78, 83, 89

Maori, 139–43, 149

Master Tuition Agreement, 70–72

McGifford, Diane, 158, 160

McKay, Doreen, 10, 21

McKay, Jim, 103

McKay, Mary Ann, 6

McKay, Patsy, 10

McKay, Stanley, 29

McKay Sr., Stanley, 9

McKie, Doug, 99

McKinnon, Catherine, 114

McLean, Jane Ann, 18, 19, 20

McManus, Pat, 45, 46–48, 72, 76, 85, 177, 178

Meadmore, Marion, 75

Memorial University, 157

Mercredi, Ovide, 176

Métis, 54–55

MIB (Manitoba Indian Brotherhood), 67–70

A Million Futures: The Remarkable Legacy of the Canadian Millennium Foundation (Cameron), 166

Mintz, Bud, 119

Miskokomon, Roberta, 134

Mokakit Indian Education Research Association, 133, 134–37

Monterey Dance Gardens, 24

More, Art, 98, 99, 100–101, 102, 108–9

Morven, Kathy, 129

Mount Currie School, 123

music in teaching, 27, 31, 35

Musqueam Nation, 147

Myran, Shirley, 121

N

Nalevykin, Shirley, 123–24

Naskapi Indians, 88

National Aboriginal Achievement Awards, 163

National Aboriginal Achievement Foundation (NAAF), 163–65

National Indian Brotherhood (NIB), 74, 77–84, 86

Native Awareness Day, 112

Native Indian Teacher Education Program (NITEP): hires VK, 98–101; launch of masters program of educational administration, 120–25; and longhouse, 147; offices of, 111–12; success of, 151; VK teaches for, 100, 107–9, 119; VK works as supervisor of, 109–10, 112–19, 121

Native languages, preservation of, 139–45, 154–55

Native resources in schools, 30, 57–60, 66, 90–91, 94–95

Native Studies programs, 126

Native teachers, training of, 56, 57, 64, 95, 116, 147, 156. *See also* Native Indian Teacher Education Program (NITEP)

New Zealand, 139–43

NIB (National Indian Brotherhood), 74, 77–84, 86

NITEP. *See* Native Indian Teacher Education Program (NITEP)

non-Status Indians, 10, 12, 17, 125

Normie's Goose Hunt (Cowel), 58

Normie's Moose Hunt (Cowel), 58

Norquay School, 23

Norway House, MB, 34, 36–40, 45–46, 65

O

O Great Creator: A Collection of Works (Spence), 155

Odjig (Daphne Beavon), 77

Okemow, Moses, 176

Olds, Beverly, 22, 23, 24, 152

Opaskwayak, MB, 88

Osborne, Helen Betty, 166

Otineka Mall, 88

P

parent-teacher meetings, 26–27, 35–36

Pedersen, George, 126–27

Pelican Rapids, MB, 56

The People's Library, 72

PhD Studies for Aboriginal Scholars (PSAS), 162–63

Philippines, 63

Poerschke, David, 110–11, 179

Policy Directions for Nurturing the Learning of Our People (report), 164

Poonwassie, Deo, 160–61, 162, 163

post-secondary education, 82–83, 157–63. *See also* graduate studies

Private Home Placement Program, 44

Program for the Education of Native Teachers (PENT), 56, 64

public schools, 70–71, 72, 79, 89–91

R

Reedy Creek, 19–20

research: and Mokakit Indian Education Research Association, 133, 134–37; and University College of the North, 159–60; VK's work in, 87–89, 139–43, 154–55

Rickerd, Don, 115

Rossville Indian Residential and Day School, 34–36, 39–40

Royal Commission on Aboriginal Peoples (1996), 145

Ryan, Joan, 99–100, 128

S

Sanderson, Sol, 84

Saunders, Adeline, 113

Sawatsky, Erna, 76

Sealey, Bruce, 59–60, 61, 77, 87, 91, 110

Selkirk, Sheena, 138, 141

Shamattawa, 59

Shead, Gordon, 59

The Shocking Truth about Indians in Textbooks (report), 73

Sinclair, Joanne, 29

Smallface Murule, Maria, 135

Smith, Cecil, 87, 89

Social Sciences and Humanities Research Council (SSHRC), 162

social studies, 59–60, 66, 72–73, 79

Spence, Ahab, 77, 112, 149, 155

Spence, Bette, 149